Brea

from Crisis to

Confidence

HOW TO RECOVER FROM A SUDDEN
BREAK-UP OR DIVORCE, AND
CREATE YOUR VIBRANT NEW LIFE

Claire Black

First published 2020

Published by Forward Thinking Publishing

The information given in this book should not be treated as a substitute for professional medical advice; always consult a medical practitioner. Any use of information in this book is at the reader's discretion and risk. Neither the author nor the publisher can be held responsible for any loss, claim or damage arising out of the use, or misuse, of the suggestions made, the failure to take medical advice or for any material on third party websites.

A catalogue record for this book is available from the British Library.

ISBN: 978-1-8380445-0-3

FOR MY WONDERFUL BOYS, LAURIE & FRASER,

AND MY LOVELY SECOND HUSBAND, PAUL.

THANK YOU ALL

Contents

CHAPTER 1

Introduction

This book is for anyone who has been shocked and hurt by the sudden break down of a relationship. It's the book I wish had existed 12 years ago, when my marriage ended very suddenly one Tuesday night in March 2008.

Perhaps you are married, or living with your long-term partner, or perhaps the relationship you believed was for life has ended without warning. When you got married or committed to your partner for the long term, you were filled with hope and optimism, and you never imagined that it might end very suddenly. And now that it has, it may have left you feeling shocked, lost, betrayed and angry – feeling a thousand different emotions all at once, and asking a million questions that may never get answered. Unless you've been there, it can be challenging to imagine how it feels to be on the receiving end of such shattering, life-changing news. I remember feeling totally at sea, lost and caught in a whirlwind of spiralling emotions, with no idea what to do, how to tell anyone, or how I would survive.

I know now that all of those feelings were normal. Divorce is recognised as one of the most traumatic experiences you can go through in life, second only to the death of a loved one. Even if it is a decision you have made slowly, logically and over time, it brings huge change, and the effects ripple out across your whole life – your home, family, friends, work, finances, your feelings about yourself and who you are.

When the relationship around which you've built your life, hopes and dreams ends out of the blue, and you weren't expecting it, it is one hell of a shock, which can leave you reeling. It's no wonder it can feel like your life has derailed.

Perhaps you feel:

- lost or rudderless
- afraid of tomorrow and what it might bring
- scared about how you will cope
- worried about how you will look after your children on their own
- angry that the person you love could do this to you
- abandoned after years of supporting your spouse to achieve his or her goals
- scared that you are financially at risk
- numb or empty
- confused about what to do
- unsure who to ask for help
- overwhelmed by the decisions ahead of you
- afraid that no-one will ever love you again
- betrayed

- depressed and vulnerable
- ashamed that you have somehow failed

If you recognise any of these feelings, then this book is for you. If you are reading this book having been blindsided by a break-up that came out of the blue, that you didn't expect or anticipate, please know that you don't have to navigate your way through a sudden break-up alone. Although it may not feel like it right now, I can promise you that it is possible to recover, to rediscover who you are, and to create a new life that gives you pleasure and joy.

I understand that might seem impossible right now. Whether you believe you can, or whether you believe you can't, I am here to hold the belief for you that you can feel happy again, that you can get over your heartbreak, and feel back in control of your life and future. I will hold that belief until you are ready to step into it yourself. I offer you hope and a promise that you will feel better, that there is light at the end of the tunnel.

Throughout this book, I will show you strategies and techniques that you can use to take care of you, move through your feelings, and focus on moving forward so that, when you are ready, you can create a new life that feels right for you.

I'll start by telling you some of my story.

CHAPTER 2

My Story

When I went through my very sudden break-up and subsequent divorce in 2008/9, it totally floored me. It felt like the end of the world, and I had no idea how to handle it, what to do, how to even begin to imagine what my life might look like next week, let alone next year, or in 5 years' time.

I had a pretty text book life until I was 35. I did well at school and studied History at university in Bristol. After university, I trained as a teacher and taught for 3 years before returning to college to study law, with the support of my boyfriend. I then worked in London for a big City law firm, and we got married in August 2000. In 2004 we had our first son, and our second followed 2 years later. All very traditional. I had never really had to face failure, adversity, or struggle to achieve anything I set my mind to.

And then, on 25 March 2008, my husband told me that he had been seeing someone else, and that for him our marriage was over. In the time it took him to say those words, my whole world crashed down around me.

The boys were asleep upstairs (they were 3 and 1 at the time), and I remember sliding down the wall, ending up sitting in a foetal position on the floor. I felt sick. I couldn't breathe. I was in shock, and my mind swirled with hundreds of questions:

- Why are you doing this to me?
- Are you leaving me to look after our two children on my own?
- How can I stop you from going out of the front door?
- But you never told me you were unhappy?
- How will I tell people about it?
- What will my family say?
- What will our friends think?
- Will our boys be ok?
- What have I done so wrong to deserve this?
- Was I that bad a wife?
- Why hadn't I seen any signs that this was coming?
- Will our children grow up in a broken home?

In the space of those few seconds, my life changed. In the days, weeks and months that followed, I faced fear, uncertainty, and so many overwhelming emotions that sometimes I felt I didn't know which way was up. One minute I'd feel sad, the next angry, and the next numb. I was confused and hurt, and I felt betrayed. Even now, the first 3 months are a blur. I lost over 2 stone in 6 weeks, I stopped sleeping well, I talked endlessly to friends on the phone, and I lived with hope for a time that I would come home one day to find his car on the drive and know that it had all been a bad dream.

If this is how you feel, I am here to reassure you that it is all totally normal.

There is hope, even when things seem to be very dark. Through those days, I found strategies to cope and handle the emotional roller coaster that I found myself on, and that is what this book is all about.

Fundamentally, I knew that I didn't want to let this beat me. I remember thinking that I didn't want to sink; I wanted to swim. I was lucky to have amazing friends and neighbours who were ready and willing to offer tea, hugs, space while I cried, and who helped me to see a way forward.

Fast forward 12 years, and the picture is different. I am happier now than I have ever been. I am confident in myself, and I know I have strategies to handle anything that life might throw at me. I love my work, which has developed organically from my own experience of divorce. My children are happy and settled, and they have a great relationship with both me and my ex. We are both remarried, and our sons spend 5 nights per fortnight with their dad. They are 16 and 13 now, and they are growing up into fabulous young men of whom we are proud – very far from the initial image I had of children from a "broken home". They have another brother at their dad's house whom they love. We have a great co-parenting relationship (most of the time!) and we work together to do the best for our boys.

When I was going through my divorce, I found it challenging to find objective, helpful and constructive advice on how to handle what was happening to me, how to deal with all the emotions I felt, and how to face the uncertain future that now stretched out in front of me, overwhelming me and filling me with fear.

It is my experience of separation and divorce that has driven me to help others going through this experience. When I look back on my experience now, I feel immensely proud of how I behaved, and how I turned things around for myself. I am here to show you that you too can do this, so that when you look back in 5 or 10 years' time, you too can feel proud of how you handled your break-up or divorce.

Throughout the book, I will share more of my story, and some of my clients' stories with you. In all of them, the names have been changed to protect anonymity, along with some of the factual details of the cases. It is vital to me that my clients trust me, that they know I have their back, and I am very grateful to all of those who have given me permission to share their stories and experiences to help you. If you would like to read some of my clients' stories, you can find them at the end of this book.

Now that you know a little bit about my story, the rest is all about you.

CHAPTER 3

My Philosophy

At the heart of my work are several fundamental beliefs, which come from both my life experience and my study of NLP and its principles. NLP, or Neuro Linguistic Programming, is a collection of models, techniques and strategies to help you understand your thought processes and behaviours, so that you can better understand yourself and others, communicate more effectively and learn new ways of thinking and being.

It isn't what happens to you that makes the difference; it is what you do with what happens to you

No matter what life throws at you, when you take the approach that what you do matters, and that what you do can change the outcome you get, you can take back conscious control of your life. You start to move from feeling like life is *happening to you*, to feeling that you have power to make changes, see choices and make decisions – that you are in charge of the outcome you get.

This might feel impossible at first, and you will probably start with small changes and shifts. Each of these small shifts will help you to focus forwards. In the early days of a separation, this might be tiny things like changing some of your routines, listening to different music, starting to notice when your thoughts spiral downwards, or deciding not to check out your ex on Facebook. Such changes might seem small, but they will have a very positive impact over time.

If you do what you've always done, you'll get what you've always got, so if what you're doing isn't working, try anything else!

Einstein is often credited with saying that "insanity is doing the same thing over and over again but expecting different results". Whether he actually said that or not, the point remains. If you keep doing the same thing, in the same way, you will keep getting the same results. When you decide to do something differently, you will get a different result.

For example, when my husband first left, I used to find that the worst parts of the day were the first ten minutes on waking, and then lying in bed at night trying to sleep. I had got into the habit of checking my phone for messages first thing in the morning, and last thing at night. Any message from my ex would be the first and last thing I saw every day. Doing this meant that I started and ended my days feeling anxious and miserable. A simple change to my routine made a massive difference.

Instead of looking at my phone I decided that I would switch my phone off at 10 pm every night, and I would not switch it on until after I had showered and had breakfast in the morning. I also bought a notebook and began to write down 3 things, last thing at night, that I was grateful for that day. I then read those through again first thing the next morning.

A small shift from looking at the negative to looking for the positive began to reframe my days.

You have all the resources you need to succeed.

Often, clients come to me feeling that their separation is happening to them, that they are not in control of their feelings, thoughts and actions. It is easy when you are in shock to forget all the skills and qualities that you have. I am here to remind you of those, and to help you see how you can apply those skills now.

Choice is better than no choice.

I am always inspired by Viktor Frankl (1905 – 1997), an Austrian psychiatrist and holocaust survivor, who wrote in his book, "Man's search for meaning":

"Life can take away everything you possess except one thing – your ultimate freedom to choose how you will respond to the situation. You cannot control what happens to you in life, but you can always control what you will feel and do about what happens to you."

All the time, you gather information about the world around you, by taking in and processing information via your senses – what you see, hear, smell, touch, taste and experience. Evidence suggests that we are all exposed to around 2 billion bits of information every second of every day. Unsurprisingly, your brain can't retain 2 billion bits of information every moment, so you organise that information in your own unique way, keeping some of it, and deleting, generalising or distorting other bits, to build up a picture of the world and how it works.

Do you ever hear your own voice inside your head? Or someone else's voice? When you build up your picture of the world, you use internal language to describe, code and give meaning to what you experience. You store memories, and create beliefs and values based on what you see, hear and sense. Those beliefs, values and experiences, then inform your everyday life and how you see the world. They influence your thoughts, your feelings and actions, and over time you develop patterns of thought and behaviour in accordance with your beliefs. Those patterns can either help or hinder you.

In NLP, we call this your "map of the world".

Your map of the world is unique to you. My map of the world will be different to yours, and yours will be different to your ex's. Our versions of reality will all be different, and we will all interpret the same event in different ways. The better we can understand our own, and others' reality, the better we can understand ourselves and others.

When you recognise and become aware of your thought patterns and beliefs, and assess whether they are helpful or not, you can change the way you see and experience the world, and consciously choose to put yourself back in the driving seat of your life.

How to use this book:

Throughout the book, I will share ideas, techniques and strategies to help you to:

- *Focus on you and take charge of your life*

Many of the people I work with are initially focused almost entirely on their ex – what he or she has done, how they are behaving, what they are doing, and what they might be thinking and feeling. Often, all of their energy is being put into trying to understand what has happened. When you focus on your ex, and your reactions to them, you give away your power. You allow them to control your thinking and feeling.

Instead, I encourage you to shift your focus. You are the only person who will always be there for you, you are the most important person in your life, and you are responsible for your own happiness and way forward. It is so important to realise this, and to take small steps towards putting your focus back onto yourself. In the early days, this will probably mean looking at how you can survive each day, so that you can build yourself back up over time. When you are ready, it will mean consciously moving your life forward in a way that you choose. I will show you ways to get over your heartbreak, build your confidence and make empowered choices.

- *Become clear*

I know how confusing and overwhelming a break-up and divorce can be, how uncertain and scary the future can seem. There will be lots of decisions to take and choices to make. It can feel mind-boggling and you might find just the thought of all those decisions paralysing. It is important that you take time to get clear around the things that scare you, and the big decisions that you need to make. It is vital to get clarity – even when what you find isn't what you wanted to see, it is better to know where you are so that you can consider your options. The decisions do not all have to be made at once. You can take your time to investigate, take advice, and make the best decisions for you and your future.

- ***Reclaim your power***

Although it may not feel like it right now, you can have power over your environment, your thoughts, your feelings, actions and your outcome. I will show you how you can shift your focus to look for opportunities rather than staying feeling stuck.

I remember my first session with one client, Annie. Annie came into the session and told me that she didn't believe she could change anything. She certainly didn't believe that she had the power to change her thoughts. She felt stuck and described herself as a prisoner in her own home, as she and her ex were still sharing their house. At the end of our session, I asked her what the most important thing was that she had realised, and she said "You showed me how I could control my mind." She left with strategies to take back some of her power, to create a safe space for herself at home, and with ideas of how she could bring some of the assertiveness she used all the time at work into her home environment. These small steps gave Annie a new sense of safety, freedom and confidence.

Claire Black

- ***See options and choices***

Reclaiming your power also means knowing what you can and can't control, and this is fundamental. Many of my clients are trying desperately to control or change the actions their ex takes, and this is always futile, and frustrating because you can't make anyone do anything. Instead, I will help you to look for options, and make choices to take small steps to move forward within your own power.

- ***Take positive steps forward***

As Martin Luther King famously said, "you don't have to see the whole staircase, just take the first step". When you are in the early days of a separation, looking to the top of the staircase can be incredibly daunting, and too overwhelming. My advice is always to break it down into small, achievable chunks. Lots of small steps taken over time add up to big leaps forward.

I am here to reassure you that it is possible to climb that staircase. The techniques and strategies that I will share with you in this book will help you to take those small steps. When you focus consistently over time on taking just the next small step forward, you will keep that forward momentum going. When you look back in just a few weeks or months, you will see just how far you have climbed.

As you go through this book, you'll see that it is interactive. There are exercises and steps to take woven into the advice that I give. The important thing is to keep looking forward. The exercises are designed to help you move from where you are now, to where you want to be in small steps – even if you are not sure what that looks like right now, remember every tiny step forward is a step in the right direction.

You can also download the exercises and techniques from the book on my website, to use along your journey.

It isn't what happens to you that matters; it's what you do with what happens to you that makes the difference

The first thing that I will ask you to do is to buy a new journal or diary that you can use as you go through this book. Many of my clients buy a lovely one, with an inspiring picture or motivational quote on the front. The trick is to buy a journal that draws you in, and that you will want to use. Perhaps it has a positive mantra on the front cover, or a picture of an animal that gives you strength. One of my clients has a book with a flamingo design all over it because it reminds her that, just like a flamingo, she can stand tall and proud.

Dip in and out of this book as you need to. Use and adapt the exercises and advice and notice what happens when you try something different. Make notes in your journal, record what you experience, and look back sometimes to see just how far you've come.

Used together, these tips and strategies can help you to move through the pain and challenges of a break-up or divorce, until you are ready to redefine yourself and create a new and vibrant life that brings you joy.

CHAPTER 4

Understanding the Healing Process

The first few months after my separation were the hardest of my life. I know now that I was going through a grieving process. Many psychologists call this the Grief Cycle, but I prefer to call it the "Healing Process", as to me that feels more positive and focused on the future.

Divorce is a grieving process, and it will be different for everyone. As you go through your break-up, you might grieve many things - the loss of your spouse/partner, the loss of the life you thought you had, the loss of a promise of a lifelong relationship, the loss of your nuclear family, perhaps the loss of extended family. Perhaps you feel that you have lost a sense of yourself, of who you are and what your purpose is. The process will be completely personal to you. Even if you have instigated your split, you will probably find yourself grieving loss, and moving through the different stages of healing. The emotions you are feeling throughout the process often reflect the stage of healing that you are in at that time.

In 1969, Swiss psychologist Elisabeth Kubler-Ross set out 5 stages of grief in her work 'On Death and Dying'. It has been generally accepted that these stages are common when people go through any kind of change that they perceive as negative in their lives – including separation and divorce. Psychologists broadly agree that there are 5 stages in the healing cycle:

These stages don't occur in any specific order, and you will undoubtedly move backwards and forwards between them. It isn't a linear thing, where you can expect to move seamlessly from one stage to the next until you finally reach acceptance. Much more likely you will find yourself circling around the stages. For me, it was more like a spiralling roller coaster, with lots of twists and turns, and changes of focus and direction. One moment I might feel so angry I could shout and scream, and the next day, or hour, I might just want to curl up and cry. You might find that the ups and downs of your feelings are unpredictable and scary.

Different people will spend different amounts of time in each stage, with varying levels of intensity. Some people get 'stuck' in one of the phases and find it hard to move towards acceptance.

Denial

In this stage, you might be thinking "This can't be/isn't happening to me". Perhaps you're hoping that you will wake up tomorrow and it will all be over. I lived in this stage for a while after my husband left. Every night I would go to sleep (if I slept at all) hoping that in the morning, I would wake up and find it had all been a bad dream, that my life hadn't really crumbled around me.

Denial and shock are how your brain reacts instinctively to protect you from the pain of a reality that you aren't yet ready to handle. It helps you not to feel totally overwhelmed. Your subconscious mind wants to keep you safe, so it refuses to believe what is happening. And that's ok, and normal.

This stage is challenging, but please be reassured; it will end.

Anger

This stage might sound like "how dare he/she do this to me!", "He/she is such a *****!", or "This isn't fair!". This is when you feel so angry you could lash out. My client Caroline once described her reactions in this stage as 'animalistic' – she felt driven by instinct and small things could trigger big reactions. Some of you may find that you get stuck in anger, and it feeds your actions and thoughts for a long time.

Anger often hides other emotions underneath – I know that when my anger flared, it was often because

I felt humiliated, hurt or rejected, or terribly sad that our children would now grow up in a "broken home" (how unhelpful is that phrase?!).

I didn't spend all that long in anger – which some of my friends found strange, given what had happened. Even now, I'm not sure why. Perhaps it was my general approach to life, and my fundamental belief that time spent being angry was time not spent focusing on how I could make things better for myself and my children. Or that time spent in anger was only punishing and damaging to me. I often use the analogy of anger being like drinking poison and then waiting for someone else to die. It just doesn't happen, and the person you are angry with often doesn't even know.

However, anger is a normal part of the healing process. It is normal to feel angry, especially if you have been hurt, betrayed, or blindsided by a sudden break-up that came out of the blue.

Bargaining

This stage is when you start trying to negotiate within your own head, or with God, the universe, or even with your ex. You might find yourself thinking "If I was a better person/slimmer/funnier/sexier, this wouldn't be happening to me", or "If I can make sure I lose weight/dress in his/her favourite clothes, he/she will come back", or "If I could just have had the courage to raise that issue earlier, none of this would have happened".

At this point, your brain is trying to come to terms with what has happened and to protect you from the underlying pain by coming up with ways to avoid it and keep you safe.

Depression

This stage is often accompanied with thoughts like "I just want to stay in bed", "I can't face this", "I can't go out there and do this", and a lack of energy to do anything. Perhaps you feel humiliated or ashamed, or that everyone is wondering what made you such a poor spouse. Please know that this too is a normal part of the healing process. Whether you have been through the sudden shock of betrayal, or a slow drawn out separation, at some point your brain will need to face the pain and anguish that it was trying to protect you from during the denial and bargaining stages. It is normal to feel low and down. It is ok to cry and it is ok to have days when you just feel you can't face the world. Sometimes it is ok to just breathe.

I remember very early on after my husband left promising myself that I would allow myself 3 months to 'wallow', and then I would 'pick myself up'. What was interesting was that after the 3 months had passed, I realised I did feel better. I had trained my brain to expect to feel better after 3 months. I had begun to notice the upsides to my situation – that I could get a babysitter and go out without consulting anyone, that I could eat ginger (my ex-husband hates ginger!), that I now had time to go running on the weekends the boys were with him without having to worry about childcare.

If you feel stuck in depression, you may want to consult your GP or a therapist to help you move through the sadness.

Acceptance

This is the stage when you start to feel at peace with what has happened, and your thoughts might include "I am ok", "I am thriving and I feel hopeful for the future". You can see a future ahead of you, and you know you will be ok. You will have started to make plans, to imagine how your new life will look, and you will start to take steps towards that new life.

Acceptance doesn't mean that you will feel happy about your separation. It doesn't mean that you have "got over it", and it is all forgotten. You will probably still feel negative emotions. Even now, I still feel twinges of sadness and regret that the marriage I thought would last forever, didn't. What acceptance means is that you can live with that, that you can look forward and create a new life that is fulfilling and vibrant, and that suits you. You may also find that you have learnt a huge amount from your divorce. I know that I have much to thank my divorce for, as it gave me an opportunity to redesign my life, to grow and enrich myself, and to model resilience to my children.

As you read this chapter, perhaps there were parts that resonated more than others? Perhaps you recognise yourself in some of my words. Wherever you feel you are on your journey, never give up hope that you will get through this.

As time goes by in a relationship or marriage, your individual lives often become intertwined like roots. It is no wonder that when such a close relationship ends, it can be painful. For a while it might feel like part of you is missing, and that hurts. The early days and nights of my separation were some of the very darkest days and nights I have ever experienced.

I found it helpful to know that I was going through a process, that what I was feeling was normal and to be expected. It also gave me the ability to believe that I would reach acceptance and feel happy again.

And so will you.

Use the technique below to work out where you are right now, and to notice how that may shift and change over time.

Where are you right now?

Take a moment to think about the different stages of the healing process and ask yourself:

- Where am I right now, today, in this moment?
- Where was I yesterday?
- Where was I last week?
- On a scale of 1 – 10, how strong are my emotions right now?
- What do you notice about how you are moving through and around the different stages?
- What do you notice about how long you tend to stay in each stage, and the changing intensity of your feelings over time?

Please do re-read this chapter as and when you need to, to remind yourself of the stages and go through the "Where are you now?" technique regularly. When you do that, and notice where you are, and how that changes from week to week and month to month, you'll start to see how you are moving through the stages. Remember, it's your journey, and your healing process, so avoid comparing yourself to others, or to how you think you *should* be feeling at any point.

Many of my clients find that they circle between two or three of the stages more than the others. And that's OK. I spent quite a long time moving between the bargaining, anger and depression stages in the first few months of my separation.

Always remember that it is ok to be exactly where you are, right now. Notice and be kind to yourself about where you are right now. As you move through this book, I'll give you lots of strategies to help you move from where you are, to where you want to be, so that by the end, you can look back and feel proud of the journey you have taken.

As you move through your break-up, it will be important that you have ongoing support, so in the next chapter we'll look at how to create your empowering support team.

CHAPTER 5

Knowing where to turn for support - Building your Network

When you are going through a divorce, I can't emphasize enough the value of having a strong support network, so that you know that you are supported in all areas – emotionally and practically.

Your emotional support network

When I was going through my divorce, my friends and family were a lifeline of support for me. In the early days I spent hours and hours on the phone to various very patient friends. I spent many of the first weekends when the children were with their dad with wonderful friends and family in various parts of the country who were always there offering a spare bed and company. On the night that my husband left, my brother drove for 3 hours, arriving in the middle of the night. My parents spent hours driving up and down the M4 to be there to help when I needed someone to look after the children while I tried to work. At a time when I felt totally lost and at sea, I felt I had people I could lean on.

Radiators or drains?

I love the analogy that people are either radiators or drains. Some people are warm and comforting, or fun and free, and they leave you feeling upbeat and better, and those are the radiators. Others are perhaps more focused on themselves, their own issues, and they bring everything back to them, leaving you feeling depleted, and those are the drains.

The people you spend time with now really matter. They can have a massive effect on your state of mind and how you feel. When you surround yourself with people who lift you up, who listen to what you need, who love you and care for you, and with whom you feel at ease and comfortable, you will feel supported. I had a brilliant local friend, who lived just around the corner from the nursery my children went to. After dropping them at nursery, I would pop in for a cup of tea and would often find myself being given breakfast. It always made me feel better, and in the very early days it meant that I actually ate something.

Try this exercise to get more clarity on who are your radiator friends:

Who are my radiators?

Next time you spend time with someone, take a moment to notice how you feel afterwards.

How would you describe how you feel after spending time with that person?

- Do you feel calm? refreshed? loved? supported?
- Or do you feel agitated? angry? depressed?

When you spend time with your best friend, do you come away feeling better or worse about your situation?

Would you like to spend more or less time with this person?

Make a list of all your radiator friends.

You may find yourself being surprised by who really steps up and becomes an invaluable friend while you go through your separation. And you may be disappointed in some friends who don't seem to know what to say, or what to do, so they say and do nothing. I will be forever grateful to those wonderful friends who really took me under their wing, who listened for hours and who helped me out in so many different ways.

Be careful who you share your darkest worries and concerns with. Spend time with those you trust, and who make you feel better. Avoid those who like to gossip or give you well-meaning but misguided advice. Cutting up your ex's clothes may feel like a great idea right now, but it won't feel so good tomorrow.

Remember that your friends and family may have strong emotional reactions to your break-up, so they are not impartial. Remember that this is your journey – whatever advice they may give, remember that they are not you. When anyone offers advice beginning with "If I were you...", remember that they aren't you, and they aren't in your shoes. They aren't the ones who will have to live with the consequences of any actions you take.

Later, I'll talk about the importance of taking some exercise each day, to get endorphins into your blood stream. Having a friend who would go for a regular walk with you will also help you to cope.

Once you have made a list of all the people in your emotional support network, you can go to your list and find the perfect person in those moments when you aren't sure what to do, or who to call.

Who's in my emotional support team?

Take a double page spread in your journal. Spend a few minutes thinking about what sort of emotional support you need right now, and who could offer that support.

You may find these questions useful to get you started:

- Who are my radiator friends?

- Who makes me feel good about myself?
- Who is good at listening without judging or telling me what to do?
- Who always has a cup of tea ready and a shoulder to cry on?
- Who makes me laugh?
- Who will go for a walk or run with me outside in the fresh air?
- Who do I trust not to talk about me with others or behind my back?
- Who do I know who has been through something like this, and come out the other side?
- Who is always ready with a hug?
- Who can I call at 2 am when it all feels too much?

Make a list of all the people in each category, and keep it where you can see it easily, or find it at a moment's notice when you're feeling low.

These people will form the basis of your emotional support team. The team might shift and move, and new people may enter it – and that's great!

Your practical support network

As important as your emotional network of support is your practical network. Having people around who can offer you support for the practical side of life helps to reduce the overwhelm that you may be feeling. Breaking your support network into sections will also help to reduce the overwhelm and make it easier for you to identify who you need to call in relation to any particular issue.

Split your practical support network into various sections: practical, legal, and financial.

Practical

When you find yourself suddenly on your own, there are times when you need practical help. I've needed all sorts of practical help over the years – from someone to help me lug out an old carpet, to someone to spend an hour with the children while I got my hair cut or help to get my car started when I left the lights on overnight. Sometimes I needed help with picking the children up, or babysitting. Or someone who would sit with me and help me sort out a pile of paperwork that I had been putting off for weeks and work out a list of people I needed to contact to let them know the situation and change the information they held – like the Council Tax office. I also found it invaluable to have someone in my team who could come along to my meetings with my lawyer, to take notes so that I didn't miss anything. Thanks Dad!

Take some time to do the exercise below, and start to create your practical support team:

Who's in my practical support team?

Take another page in your journal and take a few minutes to consider what sort of practical help you feel you need. Jot down any ideas you have about tasks that you could use some help with. Where would practical help make a real difference to your life?

Here are some questions to get you started

- Who can offer me help with the children?
- Who is organised, and could help me get started on the paperwork?
- Who understands numbers and could help me unpick my bank account?
- Who is handy with cars and tools, and could help me if things go wrong with my car or house?
- Who do I know who is good at odd jobs around the house?
- Who would be a good person to take notes for me when I meet with my legal team?

Of course, you may think of all kinds of other things that would make a difference.

Keep a list of all those people and use it when a practical task just seems too much, or you would like a helping hand.

Legal

Many people think that they need to instruct a lawyer right at the start of their separation. Whilst this might be true for some people, for many of my clients instructing a lawyer happens further down the line. Many of my clients work with me first, and I help them to choose the right lawyer for them, their circumstances and priorities. It's important that you choose the right lawyer for you and your situation

I remember the first meeting I had with my lawyer, about 6 weeks after my husband left. I wasn't really in a place to be able to give any meaningful instructions, and I certainly wasn't capable of really taking in any advice about my legal circumstances. The only sentence I really remember from the meeting was "You don't have to do anything right now". In that one sentence, she told me it was ok to wait until I was ready and knew what I wanted to achieve before instructing her, or indeed someone else. I felt instant relief at that sentence, as at the time I didn't have a clue what I wanted to do. I was emotionally overwhelmed, afraid and hurting. After the initial meeting I didn't go back for 6 months. When I did go back, I was in a much stronger emotional position to be able to handle the divorce. When I was ready, I went back to that lawyer, because that one sentence meant that I trusted her to do what was best for me, not what was best for her billing results.

I'm not suggesting that you hide away from taking steps to choosing a lawyer to act for you in your divorce – far from it. What I am saying is that it's ok to wait until you are sure that you know what you want that lawyer to do. Instructing a lawyer to start divorce proceedings when you are reeling with shock may not be the best way forward and is likely to result in an emotional and costly divorce process.

When it is the right time, make sure you choose your lawyer carefully. I would advise that you meet with at least 3 lawyers before you decide which one to instruct. Many law firms offer a free first half hour consultation, so use these to get a feel for whether you like the person, and whether you think you could work well with them.

Before you instruct a lawyer, think carefully about what your priorities are, and what skills you need that lawyer to have. If you and your ex own a shared business for example, look for a lawyer who has experience dealing with that aspect. If your ex is particularly high conflict, you may want to look for a lawyer who has a reputation for holding boundaries calmly and with dignity – not necessarily one who has a reputation as a rottweiler in court.

Ask for recommendations from friends or colleagues who have been through a divorce. If you are working with a coach like me, work through your priorities with them so that you are clear on what questions you want to ask. Take a list of your questions and priorities into your meeting. You might find it an emotional first meeting, so being as prepared as possible will help you to get the best from your meeting.

Of course, it is not mandatory to use a lawyer at all. Some people choose to use a company like Amicable, who specialise in helping clients divorce amicably without using lawyers. Others choose not to instruct a lawyer at all and elect to do their divorce online. There are an increasing number of ways to get divorced now, and the traditional route is not the only option. Whatever route you choose, make sure you do your research, and find the best route for you.

Financial

The decisions you make now may have long term effects for your financial future, so make sure you take financial advice. Many of my clients find the financial aspect of their separation very daunting.

The financial future may feel very uncertain and precarious, and it can be easy to ignore it, hope it will go away. However tempting this might be, I caution against it. Far better to have all your "ducks in a row" and to know what your situation looks like or may look like. Perhaps you feel that your financial future is very bleak, and that there is little you can do to change it. Neither of these approaches, ignoring or catastrophising, will help you feel any better.

It is overwhelming not knowing what you are facing. Once you have done your research, and gathered together your information, you will have a clear picture. If there are gaps, then you can start to think about how you might be able to fill them.

There are a growing number of financial advisers who specialise in helping people who are going through a divorce. A financial adviser can help you to get hold of all the information you need and consider your options.

There are also companies who offer assistance with budgeting and forecasting. Sometimes employing a third party to do the real nitty gritty work can relieve the stress for you and give you the clarity that you need to make decisions.

Again, choose a person you feel comfortable with, and who comes recommended if possible.

Coach/therapist

Many people make the mistake of seeing divorce as simply a legal process. I know from my own experience of divorce that it is one of the most traumatic things that can happen to you. Getting support for the emotional journey is, I believe, as important as getting the right legal advice. A coach or therapist can help you to overcome your heartbreak, take small steps to move forward, and ultimately take back conscious control of your life and move forward with confidence.

"One may walk over the highest mountain, one step at a time" – John Wanamaker. Each small step you take will take you further forward.

I know that meeting with lawyers, seeing your ex again in a mediation room or across a round table discussion, or preparing for a court hearing can be among the most stressful things you may ever have to do. Working with a coach can help you to prepare mentally and emotionally for the journey ahead, so that you feel confident, resourceful and resilient to handle whatever your divorce may throw at you.

Coaching or therapy also gives you a safe, non-judgmental space with someone qualified and experienced, in which to explore your feelings, consider options, make decisions, see possibilities, build up your confidence and resilience, and move forward positively.

It might seem easy to throw in the towel and feel that you are the victim of your separation or divorce, especially if you did not choose the road that you now find yourself on. I am here to tell you that you CAN survive this, and not only that, you can thrive and build a new life that excites you, that you find fulfilling and that is full of hope. To do that, you do need to decide to do something different and take conscious control to refocus your attention back onto you, your decisions, your life and your future. You can do it. As your coach, I will hold that belief for you until you are ready to step into it for yourself:

You can do this. You can redefine your life.

It is not what happens to you that makes the difference.

It is what you do with what happens to you.

Choose carefully. Most coaches will offer a free call to talk through where you are now and discuss options to move forward. It's important that you trust your coach or therapist, so if you can get a recommendation from a friend or from your lawyer. Don't be afraid to ask for details of qualifications or to see testimonials from previous clients.

Your support network will be a vital part of your journey towards recovery, so make sure you add to your list of supporters and refer back to it whenever you feel you need some extra back up or help.

I know that the very early days of a separation can be deeply challenging, so the next chapter will give you 5 quick and simple techniques you can use right now to help yourself to feel better.

CHAPTER 6

Surviving the Early Days

In the very early days, I know that separation can feel totally overwhelming, so this chapter is dedicated to 5 small, practical steps that you can take right now to help yourself feel that little bit better. Although there is no magic or pill you can take to get rid of all the pain right now, there are things you can do to start to turn down the volume and take charge of how you feel.

These are all things that I did in the first weeks after my husband left, and I know they work. Sometimes they might be the last thing you want to do, so I encourage you to give them a go. Practice them, and each time they will become easier.

I recently worked with a client, Andrew, whose wife had left very suddenly, taking their very young child with her. He felt incredibly overwhelmed, at the loss of both his wife and his child, and he wasn't sure how to get through even an hour of each day. Over a few sessions, we worked together to give him some simple resources that he could call on to survive this very dark time. With practice, Andrew made these techniques part of his everyday life, and they meant that he was able to stop, pause and think about how to handle the curveballs that his separation threw his way.

Chunk time

Perhaps one of the worst things about the early days for me was the feeling that I was on a roller coaster with a million different turns and twists every day. My feelings were very unpredictable - I could feel quite upbeat one minute, and then suddenly something would shift, someone would say something, or something would happen to remind me of what I had lost, and I would feel tearful or angry.

I found it helpful to divide my day into chunks. At first, dividing the day into 5 – 10 minute chunks was enough for me to handle. When you divide your day up into small, bitesize units, it helps you to live in the right now, and to focus on the next 5 minutes, rather than on a whole morning or day. It trains your mind to look at time differently, and to notice different things about how the time is passing. When you make it through 10 minutes without crying, or you notice that you spend a few minutes laughing with a friend, those are achievements to notice and give yourself credit for. Give yourself a pat on the back when you get through another chunk of time.

Over time, you can increase the chunks of time. I remember very clearly the first morning that I got through without feeling tearful, and even more clearly the first time that I laughed properly (at a puppet show at Bristol Zoo, about 2 months after my husband had left).

Sometimes even a small chunk of time can seem too much, I know. If you are feeling overwhelmed by your emotions, then taking a few moments out to bring calm to your breathing and focus on what you are physically experiencing right now can help.

Use this technique to bring calm:

Take a moment of calm

Sit comfortably on a chair with your feet resting on the floor. Breathe slowly in through your nose, and out through your mouth. As you breathe, listen to your breath going in and out. As you sit, take in the space, and notice:

- 5 things you can see
- 4 things you can touch
- 3 things you can hear
- 2 things you can smell
- 1 thing you can taste

This technique comes from Mindfulness practice, and it is designed to bring your focus back to the present and to help you to pause and experience a moment or two of calm. You may be surprised by the positive effect that taking just a few moments for your mind and body to pause can have.

You can do this anywhere, anytime, and no-one need even know. The aim isn't to make your emotions go away or push them aside – it's just to give you a breathing space for a few moments.

This technique was incredibly useful for Andrew, as it enabled him to breathe, to diminish the feelings of panic and anxiety that often rushed into his body, and to slow his thoughts down so that he could pause.

Look after your body

I can't emphasize enough how important it is to look after your body right now. It is so easy to forget to take care of your body when your mind is in turmoil. I'm talking about the basic things – food, exercise and sleep. Your body is going through a lot right now, and you need to look after it so that you have the strength to meet each day. The mind and body act together, so when you look after your body, your mind will also benefit.

Eating

Every time I looked at food for the first few weeks after my ex left, I felt sick, and even a few mouthfuls seemed too much. As a result, within 6 weeks I had lost nearly 2 stone, and had gone from a size 12 to an 8. Other people turn to food for comfort and take solace in eating sugary foods and sweets.

In the long run, neither of these approaches will help you. Your body is going through stress and it needs sustenance to keep going. The mind and body are intrinsically linked, so when you feed your body food that sustains and nourishes it, your mind will benefit. Small amounts of food eaten little and often will help to stabilise your metabolism and blood sugar levels without overwhelming them.

Avoid alcohol (tempting as it might be to drown your sorrows in a bottle of wine), junk food, sugar and caffeine, and instead choose foods that will boost your serotonin levels, like fruit and vegetables rich in vitamin C and omega-3 fatty acids.

Exercise

Have you ever noticed that taking a short walk in the fresh air can boost your mood? Breathing in fresh air brings more oxygen into your lungs, which increases energy, and encourages your body to produce serotonin and dopamine, which boost mood and wellbeing. Taking some time out of your day for a walk or run in the fresh air is proven to be beneficial to your wellbeing and state of mind.

Sleep

Many of my clients find sleep increasingly difficult when they are first facing their separation. I know I did. When your body and mind are under stress, they are on high alert, and it can be challenging to switch off enough to sleep.

It is also easy at night to let all the thoughts that you've been holding at bay all day crowd your mind, and to ask yourself circular questions to which there are no answers. You may have been able to avoid thinking about everything all day, by keeping busy. All those worries and fears come to the fore at night, as you lie in bed feeling anxious, with nothing to distract you. Your body is also tired and less resilient after holding it together all day.

If you are finding it a challenge to drop off at night, try these simple techniques to give your body as much help as you can:

- Have a routine that you follow and try to go to bed at the same time every night. I always take a cup of peppermint tea to bed, as I find it calms my mind and body, and leaves me feeling sleepy

- Turn your phone and other screens off at least an hour before bed, and leave them out of the bedroom
- Avoid caffeine in the evening
- Keep a book or diary by your bed so that if you wake in the night, or find it difficult to drop off, you can get your thoughts out of your head and onto paper
- Use the breathing technique below to help soothe your body and mind. This technique, which I still use when I find it a struggle to drop off, is based on Progressive Muscle Relaxation, developed by Edmund Jacobson in the 1930s. Don't worry if you drop off halfway through – enjoy the calm and safety that this exercise can bring you.

Breathing for relaxation

Lie in a comfortable position where you are warm and cushioned.

Breathe in and out slowly a couple of times, listening to your breath. As you breathe in, tense the muscles in your toes for 5 – 10 seconds and then release as you breathe out.

As you breathe out, imagine that you are breathing out all your stress. Imagine all your stress disappearing off into the sky and blowing away.

As you breathe in again, tense the muscles in your feet for 5 – 10 seconds, and release as you breathe out.

This time as you breathe out, imagine breathing out a soft mist in your favourite colour. The mist envelopes you and will keep you safe. Or imagine you are breathing out a bubble of safety that will surround you throughout the night.

Continue this through all the muscles in your body – through your ankles, legs, buttocks, tummy, arms, shoulders and neck. Scrunch up your face, your eyes, and imagine your stress disappearing off with each out-breath, being replaced by your soft warm mist or bubble of safety.

Notice how safe, warm and relaxed you feel now, cocooned in your duvet.

Avoid unhealthy avoidance techniques

One of my coping strategies early on was to keep busy, busy, busy. I avoided being at home on my own and decided to keep myself occupied all the time. After a few weeks of that, on top of all the stress I was already under, I was exhausted. Being in a state of exhaustion can be self-fulfilling, and it certainly didn't leave me any energy to put towards taking proper care of myself.

Other people I've worked with have thrown themselves into working long hours, drinking and partying into the small hours, exercising to an extreme, taking drugs or throwing all their energy into making their ex's life as difficult as possible.

The thing that all these strategies have in common is that they end up with you feeling exhausted and depleted. They shift your focus away from what you can do to feel better and put your focus on what you can do to squash your feelings.

One of my clients pushed himself to exercise daily to avoid his feelings – he swam, he walked miles. One afternoon he rang me in tears, having a panic attack at all the thoughts and fears that had suddenly engulfed and overwhelmed him. He had spent so much energy avoiding his thoughts and feelings that they suddenly became way too overwhelming, all at once.

After talking him through the Mindful breathing technique above, he recognised that he had been pushing his body so hard that he was exhausted. He concluded that he was unable to continue as he had been. Once he slowed down just a little, he began to be able to look more closely at his feelings, and work through them.

He also found a lovely technique called savouring, which is founded in Mindfulness and positive psychology. It encourages you to stop and notice little things that might otherwise pass you by, and which can give great pleasure. It might be the smell of fresh grass, the sound of a bird singing, the feeling of holding a mug of hot chocolate, or the warmth of the sun or an open fire or listening to a particular piece of music. Savouring encourages you to enjoy little moments of calm and pleasure, and really associate into them. Try this exercise, to soothe your body and mind and help you to move from stress to calm.

Savouring

Focus on the little thing that is giving you pleasure. Try closing your eyes and really feeling the feeling, or focus on the scent, warmth or sense of touch.

Allow yourself to become totally immersed in the experience. Be aware of your senses. What do you see, hear, feel? Really focus on the part of the experience that you are enjoying at that moment in time. Really let yourself feel it.

Share how you felt with a friend, focusing on the positive elements. Tell them what was so special about the experience and tell them how it made you feel. You could do this in the planning stage, while you are looking forward to an experience, or while it is happening, or afterwards when you are telling people about it.

Perhaps invite your friend to share the experience with you – when you both curl up on the sofa with a hot chocolate, notice how the shared experience is even better.

Take real or mental photographs or keep other things to remind you of those moments of pleasure.

Notice how having a small moment of pleasure in each day helps to lift your mood.

Protect yourself from social media

Is it tempting to follow your ex on social media, to check in with what they are doing on a daily or even hourly basis? Do your friends update you on what your ex is doing? Do you find yourself searching out his new partner and pouring over his/her pictures online, to get clues about why they chose them over you?

One of my clients used to check her ex's profile on Facebook every night before she went to bed, and when she was feeling down or angry, she would often check out what he had posted. I remember one session when she told me that she had been to a friend's house and had a lovely evening, but when she got home she had checked her ex's Facebook page only to see him out and about, smiling with his new girlfriend. All the good feelings she had nurtured by spending time with people who cared about her evaporated in a few moments. Checking your ex's activity on social media is like picking a scab that just won't heal. It will never heal if you keep poking it.

I call this "torture by social media". Every time you check out what your ex is doing you are feeding your negative emotions and keeping the emotional ties between you and your ex well and truly alive. My advice is to block, unfollow, and ask your friends not to tell you when they've seen your ex out having what looks like a great time. In this case, there is truth in the old cliché that what you don't know can't hurt you.

Sometimes stopping looking at your ex on social media can feel like an impossible task, you might even feel withdrawal like symptoms. But I promise you it will help you to feel better when you don't torture yourself with what he or she is doing.

Likewise, avoid airing all your thoughts and feelings on social media. Although it might feel great to get in all those comments offering hearts and hugs, and adding to the criticisms of your ex, again this fuels the emotional ties, and will lock you into negative emotions.

Smile

> *"Smile in the mirror. Do that every morning and*
> *you'll start to see a big difference in your life"*
> *-Yoko Ono*

Very early on in my divorce, a wise friend advised me to 'wear a smile'. She told me to consciously remind myself to smile, even when I didn't feel like it (and there were plenty of those times!).

You might think that there is very little to smile about when you're dealing with the challenges of a divorce, and I admit I was sceptical. At the time, I had no idea why smiling was such a good idea. But I tried it and found that it really did work. As a coach, I now know that there are proven physiological reasons as to why smiling is good for you. As a result, I often advise my clients to wear a smile, even though it might not feel like there is much to smile about.

So how does smiling make you feel better?

Body language and mood are strongly linked, and evidence shows that smiling or laughing, even when you do it on purpose, relaxes the facial muscles, decreases stress hormones, and calms the nervous system.

Smiling helps lower your heart rate when you feel under stress. Smiling and laughing also release endorphins into the body. These hormones trigger a positive feeling of wellbeing in the body, and act as analgesics, reducing the feeling of pain. If you smile often enough, you will rewire your brain to make positive patterns, which helps you to have more energy, see more possibility and increase self-confidence. Smiling helps you to self-medicate and heal.

Try these techniques to remind yourself to smile and release those endorphins:

> **Smile!**
>
> Set an intention to smile as often as possible. Get up every morning with the intention of wearing a smile today. If you need to, plaster on your smile.
>
> Stick post-it notes on your mirrors, and on your fridge to remind you to smile. Put up pictures of people who make you smile.
>
> Do things that you know will make you smile or laugh.
>
> Look for opportunities to do things that you know give you pleasure. Watch a funny movie. Go and see your favourite comedian perform a stand-up act.
>
> Spend time with friends that you love and who want to encourage you on your journey.
>
> Take your children out for the day, to run in the woods or on a beach.
>
> Do an activity that you know gives you a moment of calm.

Andrew found this particularly helpful. In our first session together, I asked him what he enjoyed doing, and what gave him pleasure. He told me he lived by the sea and would often take a walk down **at** the beach with his camera to take pictures of the waves and the coastline. As he talked, his face lit up, he smiled, and his entire body language shifted. He became animated and his voice took on a new energy. One of the actions on his action plan from that session was to take a walk every day by the sea. Now he calls this "Back to Basics", and a walk on the beach is his go-to technique when things feel a bit too much.

These simple techniques are designed to help you start to feel that you have some small level of control over your day, and over your body and mind. As you move through the next chapters, I'll help you add to these so that you can really take back your power and focus on taking positive steps forward.

The next chapter will look at how you can shift your focus away from your ex and your situation, and back onto you.

CHAPTER 7

Shifting your Focus onto You

You may not be in a situation of your choosing right now, and you may be feeling all kinds of emotions, and thinking all kinds of negative thoughts. Fundamentally, though, what you do next will have huge effects on your life.

When my husband left, I decided early on to 'allow myself to wallow' for 3 months. During that time, I let myself cry, I talked non-stop to my friends about how I felt, how unfair it all was, and how sad and bereft I felt. But I realised that this wasn't really helping me. I knew deep down that I needed to do something different. I needed to take back some control over my life, and shift my focus away from my ex-husband, and onto me. I wanted to swim, not sink. I wanted to survive, not drown. I didn't want my separation to define me – as that would hand all the power over to him.

You too have the choice to let your break-up define you, or to consciously put yourself in the driving seat of your life and decide to do things differently. To do that, you need to act, make changes, and shift your focus away from your ex, and onto you. You are the most important person in your life, the only one who can really affect changes in your life. Your ex is no longer responsible, you are.

That sounds easy doesn't it? I know it is challenging, so I'm going to show you some small steps that you can take right now, to start to take back your power over your thoughts, your feelings and your life.

Use your breath to bring calm

In those moments when your brain feels overwhelmed with a thousand thoughts and questions, your breath is one of the most powerful tools you have at your disposal. And it's a resource that is ALWAYS with you. With breathing you can slow your heart rate, calm your thoughts and take time to think. When you breathe slowly and deeply, you bring oxygen into your bloodstream and your brain, and it will help combat the feelings of overwhelm.

I often tell my clients that their breath is more powerful than their thoughts. Sometimes they don't believe me at first – but it's true. Thoughts are exactly that – thoughts. They are no more than our brain's interpretation of what is happening. They are not true; they are just thoughts. Using your breath, you can overpower swirling thoughts.

Try this and see how it feels.

Your breath is more powerful than your thoughts

This exercise can be done anywhere, anytime, whenever you feel stressed or anxious.

- STOP!
- Breathe in through your nose while you count slowly to 5.
- Hold your breath and count to 2.
- Exhale completely through your mouth while you count to 8.
- As you breathe out, listen to your breath and imagine that you are breathing out all your stress and anxiety, and turning it into a soft mist in your favourite colour, that envelops you and will keep you safe.
- Repeat x 3.

Notice what happens when you count and listen to your breathing. Your brain cannot count and think at the same time so your thoughts no longer swirl around - your breath has overpowered them.

Notice how much calmer you feel.

Notice your inner voice

In the early days of a break-up, it is easy to look back, find fault and blame yourself. How often do you find yourself thinking, or hearing the little voice inside your head saying, things like "I should have....", "I ought to have....", or "If only I'd....", "Why didn't I...."?

During the early days of my divorce, I blamed myself for not being attentive or loving enough towards my husband, for devoting too much time to the children, for nagging too much, for not being funny/sexy/slim enough. Clients have told me that they feel disappointed in themselves that they didn't see their divorce coming, or that they feel stupid for not doing something sooner, or that they feel they chose their partner badly. Sound familiar?

The way you talk to yourself is hugely powerful. It has a massive impact on your self-esteem and confidence. It's hard to be happy or hopeful when someone is being mean to you all the time. It's doubly hard when the mean person is inside your own head. The good news is that you have the power to change the voice inside your head.

What is this 'inner voice'? It's those little thoughts that pop into your mind, that perhaps tell you that you deserve this, that you weren't good enough, that you won't be able to cope, that it's all your own fault. It might be your own voice, or it could be someone else's voice. It might feel like the voice is sitting on your shoulder, or you might hear echoes of words that have been said to you in the past.

The first step to changing anything is to become aware. Start to notice the way you speak to yourself, and the thoughts that repeat in your mind. When you notice critical thoughts, write them down and really notice how you are talking to yourself, and whose voice it is that is troubling you.

I learnt the following short, but hugely powerful exercise, early on in my NLP coaching course and it has had a profound effect. It reminds me of the scene in Harry Potter when the students are required to face the bogart - a magical creature that turns into your worst fear. In the book, Harry and his peers learn that the only way to defeat the bogart is to turn it into something funny. You too can change your inner voice so that it no longer has power over you.

Next time you hear that little inner critic coming out to play, try this exercise.

Challenge your inner voice

You could do this inside your head, or out loud, or take a piece of paper and write your answers. Or get a friend to run through it with you, asking you the questions.

- Notice the voice and hear what it is saying to you.
- Whose voice is it? Is it your voice? Is it your ex's voice? Is it someone else's voice?
- What does it sound like? Where is it? Is it inside your head? On your shoulder? Somewhere else?
- Does it have a physical form – do you imagine the person, or remember a scene?
- How useful is that voice to you? Is it helping you?
- How much difference would it make if you could change that voice?

- Now change the voice and/or the scene. If the voice is loud, make it quieter. If it is high, make it low. If it is behind you, bring it in front of you. Try moving it further away, or higher and lower.
- Imagine you could turn the voice into a ridiculous voice – make it talk like Donald Duck, or Minnie Mouse, or turn it into a whisper that's so quiet you barely know it's there.
- Imagine that you can also change the scene. If the voice has a shape, change it, make it smaller and yourself bigger.
- Notice how you can control the voice inside your head, and know that next time it pops up, you can do the same again – or perhaps you can even throw it away entirely.

I used to have a little voice inside my head that told me that any partner I ever had would leave me, based on my past experiences. It was a voice based on fear, but it wasn't helping me! It meant that I found it difficult to trust, and I was always looking for signs that partners would leave. It meant that I was scared to stand up for myself sometimes, in case doing so made my partner leave. And it also meant that sometimes I would do something or ask a question to test my partner's loyalty to me. When I did this exercise, I took that voice out of my head, and imagined that it turned into a powerless whisper that I could simply blow away out of the window and into the wind. I can honestly say that the voice that told me everyone would leave me has now gone.

One of my clients used to hear her ex-husband's voice in her head all the time, telling her how useless she was, and how disappointed he was in her. He appeared in her mind as a looming shadow that blocked out the light. She used this technique to turn her ex into a squeaky mouse, which was much smaller than her, so small that his shadow no longer blocked any light. She changed his voice so that it was high and squeaky and ridiculous, and found that it no longer had such a hold on her.

Be kind to yourself

The one constant person in your life is you. Other friendships and partnerships shift, they come and go as life develops and changes. So, it's important to treat yourself kindly, and to talk to yourself with love, care and compassion. Talk to yourself as you would to your best friend. Know that you can learn to give yourself the love and support that you need.

Notice the sorts of questions that you ask yourself in your mind. Are they helpful? Are they kind? Would you ask your friend any of the questions that you are currently asking yourself?

Your mind is like Google, it answers the questions you ask it!

I often listen as clients tell me they have no time to be kind to themselves, or that taking time to look after themselves is selfish. I absolutely, but kindly, disagree! When you take time to be kind to yourself, your mind and body are being soothed – and that is exactly what you need right now.

Use this exercise to practice talking to yourself with kindness, as you would to a friend:

Talk to yourself as you would talk to your best friend

Once you have taken control of that inner voice, you can replace it with a voice that asks more supportive, kinder and more compassionate questions, like:

- What would my best friend say to me right now?
- Who might be the best person to help me with this?
- How can I best care for and comfort myself right now?
- Who from my support network would give me the message I need right now? What would they say or do?
- What have I done that I am proud of today?
- What do I need right now?

Now imagine that you can float out of your body and look down on yourself with love and compassion, as if you were your own best friend, or perhaps your guardian angel. Imagine that you can beam down a ray of pure love and support, that surrounds you below with light and warmth and whatever you need right now.

- What special wisdom or nugget of advice would you give yourself?
- What gift would you give yourself right now?

Be open to receiving whatever message or gift you might have, imagine yourself receiving it and hold it close to your heart to give you strength.

When I did this exercise with Andrew, he said that his angel gave him permission to rest, to be peaceful, to trust in the universe's plan, and to know that "this too shall pass". He realised that he was tired from pushing himself, and when he was tired he tended to catastrophise. He took himself out for a walk along the beach and bought himself a kite so that he could feel the power of the wind.

For you, being kind and acting as your own best friend might mean reminding yourself of how much you achieved today, or that you always try your best, or that you are a kind and patient parent. It might mean allowing yourself to feel your sadness and have a good cry or forgiving yourself for any mistake you might feel you have made.

The more you use and practice these techniques, the more powerful they will become until eventually they will be second nature.

Remind yourself of your good qualities

It is easy in a relationship to lose sight of who you are, to muddle your characteristics together with those of your partner, to lose a little of your individuality, to mould yourself to fit in with them, to compromise. This can happen with simple things, like the kind of food you want to eat, the programmes you watch on TV, the music you listen to, how you prefer to socialise.

And it can also happen with merging who you are. You may become part of a "we" rather than feeling you are an "I". When I went to lots of weddings in my 20s, one of the most popular readings was from Captain Corelli's Mandolin:

> "*Those that truly love have roots that grow towards
> each other underground, and when all the pretty
> blossoms have fallen from their branches, they find
> that they are one tree and not two.*"

That's all very well and lovely, but it doesn't really help when that relationship breaks down, and you aren't sure what is you anymore, and what is them. Untangling those roots can be a painful journey.

The first step is to remind yourself of what makes you the person you are. What are your qualities? What makes you special? Take a page in your diary, and take some time to think about your qualities:

What qualities do I have?

In your journal, write down:

- 5 positive words that describe you
- 4 things that your best friend loves about you
- 3 things that you do well or know you are good at

Write your list out and stick it up where you can see it.

Sometimes, clients tell me that they aren't sure what their qualities are, and they struggle to think of positive words to describe themselves. When I first tried to write down 4 things my best friend loved about me, I found it challenging to say the least. My self-esteem was on the floor, I was wondering whether I was loveable at all, and I struggled to think of any qualities that I possessed.

If this is you, take a comfortable seat, and close your eyes. Breathe deeply a few times and imagine that your best friend is sitting next to you, full of support and caring, compassion and love. Imagine yourself asking them what it is they love about you. You may be surprised at what you hear.

Or you could actually ask them! A few weeks after the break down of my relationship, I plucked up my courage and messaged 5 of my closest friends and asked them to tell me what they thought my 3 best qualities were. I figured these people were my friends, so they must like me for a reason! I was wonderfully surprised by the responses. My friends all listed more than 3 qualities they felt I had, and they told me unanimously that I am loyal, friendly, a good listener, kind, caring and honest.

I printed the messages out and composed myself a statement that I typed out in big pink letters. I stuck a copy on both my fridge and the mirror behind my bed. It stayed there for the next four years:

I am kind, loving, caring, honest, loyal, friendly and I am a good person. I love my children. I like laughing, smiling and being with my friends. I am a valued friend.

Whenever I saw it, I was reminded of my good qualities. I found that I could remind myself of my qualities every time I started thinking the negative, self-blaming thoughts I had around my divorce.

Create your own affirmations

An affirmation is a positive statement of emotional support or encouragement that you can use to counter-act negative thoughts or feelings. It reminds of your good qualities and values, that you can use to challenge the inner voice and rebuild up self-belief. Affirmations need to be positive, simple, specific, and to start with "I am". They need to be dynamic and powerful.

These are some examples that I use for myself:

- I am kind.
- I am honest.
- I am caring.
- I am loyal.
- I am funny.
- I am genuine.
- I am good at listening.
- I am a good friend.
- I am resourceful.

It's time now for you to create your own affirmations, from the list of qualities that you created above.

Create your own affirmations

Go back to your list of qualities and turn each statement on your list into an affirmation that starts with "I am ....". Make sure each affirmation is positive and powerful.

Write those affirmations on post it notes, and stick them up around your house, on the fridge, on the bathroom mirror – anywhere you will see them and be reminded.

Look for evidence to support your affirmations – for example, if one of yours is "I am kind", make it your goal today to look for evidence that this is true, and jot those examples down.

You could also stand in front of a mirror and say your affirmations to yourself first thing in the morning, and last thing at night, or whenever you feel you need a boost. So, I might stand in front of the mirror, facing myself, and say "I like Claire because I am kind and honest. I am a good friend, and I am genuine".

As you become more comfortable, change your affirmation to "I love you because you are fun and kind, and good at listening and laughing".

If you find your inner voice arguing back, go back to the Challenge your Inner Voice exercise, and run through it again, turning that voice of doubt into something funny or silly that will have less power over you.

Do things that make you feel good about yourself

I know how easy it is to focus on the negatives when you're going through a break-up. When your life is in a state of transition and change, it is normal to feel afraid, to worry, and to look for all the things that could go wrong. When I was first going through my break-up, I remember there were times when it felt like the pain might never end. My body's response to all the stress was to develop IBS type symptoms and headaches. I found it hard to eat, difficult to sleep, and a challenge to stop the worries swirling around my head.

When you are in a state of high stress, your body is hardwired to produce increasing amounts of cortisol, the stress hormone. It is a natural response to what the brain perceives as threat. This is fantastic when you are facing imminent danger, like a car driving towards you at speed, or a big dog snapping at you when you're out for a walk. The hypothalamus, the part of your brain responsible for releasing hormones, will react to the threat, and prompt your adrenal glands to release hormones including cortisol and adrenalin. This will increase your blood pressure, numb your digestive system, and enable you to move quickly away from the immediate danger. Once you've moved away, the response dies down.

The problem with separation and divorce is that your body may be on high alert all the time, releasing more and more adrenalin and cortisol into your system, in response to the stress you feel under.

It's important to do what you can to counteract all of this by doing things that you enjoy, and that encourage your body to produce other hormones and endorphins like serotonin and dopamine. These are often collectively called the "happy hormones". They counter some of the effects of the high levels of cortisol that are produced by stress and worry and trigger positive feelings. They can help reduce your perception of pain and increase feelings of calm. Even when you really don't feel like it, getting out and doing something that you know you enjoy can turn your day around. It can move you from stress to soothing.

Create your own list of activities that help you move from stress to soothing:

Moving from stress to soothing

- Brainstorm all the activities that give you pleasure and satisfaction, or that help you to relax. Write down anything, however crazy it might seem.

- Choose at least 3 of the activities on your list and commit to doing them within the next month.
- Turn your commitment into a concrete plan to do those things.
- Write the activities you have promised to do on post it notes and stick them up around the house or write a list and stick it to your fridge.
- Remind yourself that you deserve it.
- Notice what activities make the biggest difference to you and do more of them!

The activities on your list don't have to be expensive, or time consuming. What is most important is that YOU enjoy them. Go back to your support network too and commit to doing some of those things with your friends and family.

My list included things like the first cup of tea of the day, playing music loudly in the car, cycling in the sunshine, singing, roller coasters, and exploring new places and cultures.

Now I have a Teasmaid, so I have tea on tap next to my bed and I cycle regularly with a fantastic group of people I have met through my local spin studio. I indulge my love of speed and adrenalin by visiting theme parks with my kids (I am lucky they share this love!). I turn the music up loud to sing in the car whenever I can. Holidays are my major expenditure every year, so that I can satisfy my love of exploration.

Show yourself that you care about you

Set aside some time every day to show yourself that you care. It doesn't matter what you do so long as it is something that makes you feel good. By doing this you are showing yourself that you love and respect yourself, and that your well-being and happiness are important. By treating yourself well, you also show others how you expect to be treated.

Again, this doesn't have to be expensive or time consuming. Buy some lovely new bubble bath and take a soak, go for a walk in the sunshine, or sing along to your favourite feel-good song. Buy yourself flowers or spend 20 minutes reading your favourite book.

When you use these techniques, you are taking responsibility for your own feelings and putting yourself where you belong – at the centre of your own life.

You are important, and you are worth it

Notice as you use the techniques how things begin to feel different. You will increase your ability to rely on yourself, trust your own decisions and intuition, and comfort yourself when things are tough. You will know that you will be ok, as you have tools to handle whatever life may throw at you.

Now that you have started to shift your focus on to you, take some time to notice how that feels, and what difference it makes. Notice what makes the biggest difference for you and do more of that!

In the next chapter, we'll look more closely at your emotions, and how you can start to identify them, face them head on, and move through them.

CHAPTER 8

The Emotional Rollercoaster - How your Emotions can Help You

"Don't be afraid to cry. All good things grow from water. Tears allow the heart to grow stronger."
-Allison Pescosolido

Going through any break-up is a hugely emotional time, and it is normal to feel a wide range of different emotions on an hourly or even daily basis When that break-up was very sudden or unexpected, it really can feel like you are on a roller coaster that just doesn't stop, and you keep going around and around the same loops, without any sense of being in control. It can be disorientating, overwhelming and frightening.

When I was getting divorced, I found the rollercoaster of emotions exhausting, and small things could easily tip me over the edge. I found my feelings confusing, as they seemed to shift every day, every hour, even minute by minute. I've listed just some of the feelings I had here:

- Afraid
- Angry
- Resentful
- Lonely
- Overwhelmed
- Disappointed
- Regretful
- Hurt
- Shocked
- Guilty
- Relieved
- Worried
- Vulnerable
- Scared
- Helpless
- Hopeless
- Betrayed
- Devastated
- Sad
- Exhausted
- Confused
- Numb

As you can see, the feelings were intense and sometimes contradictory, so it's no wonder I was confused. I felt them physically as well as in my mind, and I often felt an uncomfortable knot of tension in my stomach. I had headaches and occasionally I was physically sick. I started to suffer with IBS type symptoms, which gave me even more to worry about when I went out.

Sometimes I tried to push my emotions to one side, to ignore them, and hoped they would go away on their own (they didn't!). Or I tried to keep them at bay by keeping busy - and ended up wearing myself out. And of course, the emotions didn't disappear. Instead they often came back to bite me on the bum, and it would usually be just when I didn't want them to.

Perhaps you recognise some of the emotions I have listed above? Maybe you too are confused by the daily/hourly ups and downs in your feelings right now? If you are, know that you are not alone. You may find it helpful to put a tick by any of the emotions that you recognise and add any others of your own. Or perhaps take a page in your diary and write a list of all the emotions that you have felt over the past weeks and months.

Like me, you will probably experience a myriad of feelings, and they will probably ebb and flow from hour to hour, day to day. Sometimes you might not really know how you feel, or you might just feel numb and empty. No wonder it's confusing! Remember to be kind to yourself, and to do things that help you to soothe your mind and body.

Let me reassure you that whatever emotions you are feeling, they are normal. In fact, they are useful, and allowing yourself to feel them will help you to move closer to healing.

How your emotions are useful

Paul McKenna and Hugh Willbourn's book, "I can mend your broken heart" contains a wonderful section about emotions, in which they explain what our emotions can show and teach us:

"An emotion is a bit like someone knocking on your door to deliver a message. If the message is urgent, it knocks loudly. If it is very urgent it knocks very loudly. If you don't answer the door, it knocks louder and louder and louder. It keeps knocking until you open the door. Then it delivers its message. As soon as you understand even part of it, it becomes part of your self-understanding. And that is part of yourself. So you are changed and your emotion does its job."

Your emotions are your body's instinctive way of communicating with you. They are your body's unconscious response to events, either internal or external. They give you information about what you are experiencing. They let you know when something is wrong, or hurting, or needs to be examined. They encourage you to act and to make decisions.

Ignoring your feelings or trying to bury them will, in the long run, be damaging to your health as those emotions may remain stuck, keeping you feeling stressed, out of control and powerless. Being in a constant state of stress will maintain the flow of cortisol around your body, so that you feel in a state of high alert all the time. Burying your emotions takes up valuable energy that you could be using to nurturing yourself and better understanding your feelings and desires.

Your emotions can influence your state of mind, and your actions. When you feel a strong emotion, do you find yourself reacting instinctively? Your body might react physically, so your heart might beat faster, your face might go red, perhaps you begin to sweat, or your tummy ties itself in knots. Your inner voice might pipe up at this point too. Or perhaps you find yourself bursting into tears suddenly as waves of grief wash over you.

Sometimes, your emotions may be so strong that you struggle to manage your reactions to them. You go from feeling to action in the blink of an eye. Have you ever had one of those moments when your emotions "got the better of me"? I vividly remember shouting (swearing actually) at my ex-husband in the street shortly after our separation. My anger and upset at a small comment he made flicked a switch inside me, and I behaved in a way that I later found embarrassing. I went straight from feeling to acting in milliseconds.

I now understand that what was happening in that moment was that my emotions were hijacking my logical brain. Scientists now understand that there is a tiny part of our brain that is responsible for our emotions, and our survival instincts. It is often called the "reptilian brain" or "emotional brain", and it is responsible for reacting to the conditions you are experiencing. It can overpower the logical part of your brain, the neo-cortex.

When we experience something that triggers an emotional response, the emotional brain sends signals to the rest of our body to react, releasing hormones like adrenalin and cortisol when we feel threatened or afraid, and dopamine and serotonin when we feel happy and relaxed. It is instinctive, and the intention of the brain is to enable us to survive. All very useful when you are crossing the road, you see that a large lorry is careering towards you, and you need a shot of adrenalin to enable you to run out of the way. The flood of hormones overpowers the logical brain, and you act quickly and instinctively. At those moments, the last thing you need is for your logical brain to be in control, so that you stand still considering all your options, thinking through all the possible consequences, and coming up with the best option for action. In the time it took to think through all that, you'd be hit by the lorry.

My immediate reaction to the small comment my ex had made was anger. It raced through my brain, sent adrenalin to my body, and I shouted the first thing that came into my head. In fact, once I looked at what had happened more closely, my angry reaction was due to underlying hurt, fear and a sense of betrayal. My emotional brain reacted to the threat that it sensed, it sent a flood of adrenalin through my body, and I reacted instinctively, without thinking.

The more that you become aware of and feel your emotions, recognising them, and understanding why they have arisen, you give yourself the opportunity to choose the best way to react. You'll be on the path to acceptance and healing. Remember that there are no "good" or "bad" emotions, and your emotions can be challenging or uncomfortable. They can also come and go and shift as the day goes on. Some might be fleeting and last a few seconds, whilst others may linger and affect your mood for a longer period.

The first step is always to become aware, so I encourage you to start to notice your feelings and name them. Acknowledging them is the first step to reducing their hold over you and your thoughts and actions.

Many of my clients find this emotions wheel, developed by Australian pastor Geoffrey Roberts, helpful to identify their feelings:

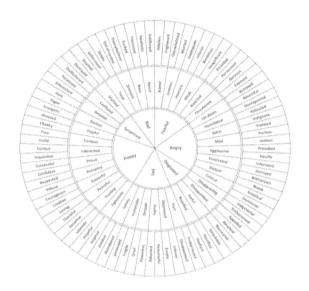

Using the emotions wheel if you need to, start to identify your feelings and making a note of them in your diary.

Identify your feelings

On a fresh page in your journal:

- Write down your emotions as you feel them.
- How strong is each emotion on a scale of 1 – 10?

- What happens to your body when you feel that emotion? Really notice how that emotion feels – where do you feel it? Can you describe what it feels like?
- Is there anything underlying your emotion? For example, if you feel angry, that might mean that underneath you feel frustrated, or humiliated, or let down. A feeling of fear might be covering anxiety about a particular event, or a feeling of overwhelm or worthlessness.
- Ask yourself what triggered that emotion. Where were you when you felt it? What just happened?
- Remind yourself that:
  o It is OK to feel this way
  o This too shall pass
  o I have all the resources I need to handle this

You could share your feelings with a good friend or someone close to you, or perhaps start to keep a diary. Writing down or sharing all your emotions, fears, worries and concerns helps to get the feelings out of your head.

"Journaling is like whispering to oneself and listening at the same time"- Mina Murray, Dracula

Once you have identified your feelings, and worked out which ones are the strongest, it's time to feel them – not to stay stuck in them, but to start to move through them and emerge the other side feeling better. Trying to ignore or squash your emotions right now isn't your best course of action. Remember it is ok to feel angry, or betrayed, or sad. It is ok to want to shout, or to burst into tears. When you are aware of your feelings and allow them to flow, you can start to move through them, rather than keeping them stuck inside. Rather than bottling them up, you can learn to surf them, and diminish their power over you.

I have adapted the 'surf the emotions' technique below from one I learnt from Francine Kaye's book, "The Divorce Doctor". I like the analogy of your emotions being like a wave, with you riding the emotion as a surfer might. When a surfer tries to go through, under or around the wave, the chances are he will be knocked off, thrown around under the water, or taken over by the force of the wave. Instead, like the surfer, your aim is to move with the wave, to use it to reach the shore and dry land.

Here are the steps to take:

Surf your emotions

When you feel a wave of emotion coming towards you, find somewhere quiet and comfortable to sit or lie down, if you can.

Imagine that you are a surfer, paddling out to meet the wave as it moves towards you.

As the wave of emotion gets closer, imagine that you are turning your board, to ride the wave into the shore. Allow the wave to get closer. Don't fight it. Name it and notice how it feels.

> Ride the wave in the direction it is already going. Remind yourself that it is moving towards the beach, and to safety. Allow yourself to feel without resisting. You might want to cry, or shout or hit pillows. So long as it is safe, do whatever you need to do right now to ride the wave to the shore.
>
> As the emotion you are feeling begins to die down, and it will, imagine that you are coming towards the shore. Imagine that the wave breaks and you land on soft sand. Breathe slowly in and out, feeling the sand beneath your feet, and the sun on your face.
>
> Rest for a few minutes and allow your breathing to return to normal.
>
> Notice how it feels to know that now you have got to the shore, you are safe and warm.

What do you notice about how you feel now? You might feel exhausted, tired, wrung out, relieved that it's over. I found that when I let my emotions out, they diminished in their power over me. The act of allowing the emotions to flood out gave me a release and sense of relief that all the busyness in the world could never give me.

Now that you can identify your emotions, and have given yourself permission to feel them, it's time to start thinking about how to diminish the hold that those emotions might have on you even further.

The next chapter will give you suggestions and ideas about how you can reduce the impact of those emotions, and give you tools to start to move beyond them and move positively towards healing and recovery.

CHAPTER 9

Turning Down the Temperature on your Emotions

Now that you've identified how or what you are feeling, it's time to look at how you can start to reduce the temperature of those feelings or turn down the volume on them when they arise. Once you can do this, you will be able to take back control over your thoughts and reactions. Long-term, you'll be able to see everything differently.

I have learnt from experience that you can control your mind and your emotions, and you can turn down the volume or temperature on any strong negative emotions you may be experiencing right now. When you have power over how you feel, you can change how you think and act, and that will change the results you get. If you're reading this thinking "Yeah right, I can't do that", let me reassure you. It is possible to change how you feel, and it will change your results. I know because I have done it myself, and I've helped dozens of my clients to do it for themselves.

This chapter will give you techniques and strategies to help you when you feel those emotions rising, or something happens that throws you.

As always the first thing to do is breathe slowly to get oxygen back to the emotional part of your brain – the part that is reacting to what is happening. Use the "Take a moment of calm" technique from Chapter 6, or "Your breath is more powerful than your thoughts" exercise in Chapter 7 to help you.

Your mind and body act together – so if you change what you do or how you think, you can change how you feel

The mind and body act as one system. What happens to one affects the other. When your mind is full of swirling thoughts, it is a challenge to get your body to feel relaxed. When your body is full of tension and stress, it is a challenge to think calmly.

Let's look first at how you can change what you are doing to change how you feel.

Change what you DO

"If you want to change your emotional state, start by changing your physical state" –Tony Robbins

How you carry your body will affect how you feel. Tony Robbins is brilliant at changing his physical state to change his emotional state, and you can do this too. You may be surprised by how some very simple changes in how you hold your body can affect your feelings.

Next time you go for a walk, look up. Take in the horizon rather than looking at the ground and notice how it influences how you feel. Looking up and taking in the horizon will give you a wider, more open view, helping you to be open to possibilities, rather than constrained by looking down to the floor.

Try this exercise to shift your feelings very quickly – in the blink of an eye in fact!

Change how you feel in the blink of an eye

Sometimes all that is needed to kickstart a change in mood or state very quickly is to change your physiology. Try any of the following or do something else that appeals to you!

- Stand up tall, raise your arms in the air with your hands outstretched and put a massive grin on your face.

- Do 5 star jumps or leg kicks.

- Stand up, consciously roll your shoulders back and hold your head up high.

- Stand up and shake your body all over – your arms, legs, torso, head.

- Imagine you are Superman and strike a power pose.

- Take 2 minutes out to skip around your garden.

- Tell yourself a joke that always makes you smile or laugh.

- Dance or clap as you listen to a song that always cheers you up. My favourites are Katy Perry's Roar, or Walking on Sunshine by Katrina and the Waves.

- Breathe deeply, whilst reminding yourself of all you have achieved, and feel that breath reaching every part of your body, taking its power with it.

Doing any of these will break the power of a negative state, leaving you free to choose a more resourceful one. Sometimes, it can be a challenge to remember to do these things, so try wearing an elastic band on your wrist, and pinging it when you notice yourself spiralling downwards, as a reminder to do something, anything, to change how you feel in the blink of an eye.

Once you know how to break your negative state by changing how you feel in the blink of an eye, you can take this further, and make permanent and lasting changes to how you hold and use your body, so that you can access your own strength and resourcefulness whenever you need it.

The next two techniques are designed to help you notice how the way you stand and move can change the way you feel and hold your body, first by noticing and modelling how others use their bodies to help how they feel, and then by using your own experiences and resources to build up your confidence.

Model someone who behaves the way you want to

Have you ever noticed the difference between how someone who feels sad or nervous holds their body, when compared to someone who feels happy or confident?

Take a moment to recall someone you know who is always down, or low, or under confident:

- How do they stand?
- How do they sit?
- How do they move?
- How do they talk?
- What sorts of words do they use?
- What do they talk about?

Now think about someone who you know who always seems to be happy, or confident, or whatever feeling it is you would like to feel more of:

- How do they stand?
- How do they sit?
- How do they move?

- How do they talk?
- What sorts of words do they use?
- What do they talk about?

What do you notice about the way their bodies reflect their feelings? How does their way of talking and standing reflect their approach to life? What happens when you try moving, talking and standing like they do?

What could you model in their behaviour that would work for you?

Try it out and see what happens!

I use the next NLP technique a lot with clients to help them associate into the positive feelings that they want more of, that will help them to move forward confidently and with belief in themselves.

Circle of Power

- Remember a time when you felt one of your negative emotions - perhaps sad, angry or low. Take a few moments to remember how you hold your body when you feel that emotion. Notice how the way you hold your body reflects your inner feelings.

- How would you prefer to feel instead? You could write a list of all the feelings you would rather have instead. For example, do you want to feel confident? strong? empowered? happy?

- How much difference would it make if you could feel those positive feelings whenever you wanted? What would you be able to do? What might be possible?

- Recall a time when you felt that positive feeling. Make sure it is a really strong example. Take a few moments to associate into that feeling. How did you hold yourself? How did your body feel? What thoughts did you have?

- Imagine that on the floor in front of you is a circle of light in your favourite colour. Inside that circle, anything is possible, and you can be whoever you need to be. As you remember yourself acting in that positive way, step into the circle and take up a body position that brings that wonderful feeling back. Feel that feeling flowing through your body, notice how much stronger it makes you feel, and notice how you feel differently now. Know that you can step into that feeling whenever you choose!

- Do this with each of the positive feelings you want to have instead. Practice stepping into your circle, with that feeling and focus. Notice how you can step into feeling confident, or strong, or empowered with one step.

If you struggle to remember a time when you felt the emotion you want to feel more of, think of someone you know who embodies that feeling, and think about how they hold their body. How do they stand? How do they move? How do they sit? Practice standing and moving in that way, and step into the circle when you feel it strongly yourself.

I know that some of you will probably be questioning whether this will work. If you don't believe, humour me and give it a go, just once or twice. You can always go back to how you were standing and moving before – it's your choice.

Change how you THINK

Changing how you think may sound really challenging, especially if you are in the midst of a separation, and you find yourself asking yourself the same sort of questions over and over again. I remember asking myself questions like:

- Why is this happening to me?
- What did I do to deserve this?
- Why is my life so difficult?

Sara Davison calls these questions "hamster wheel questions" – a very apt description. They circle around, but never take you anywhere new or helpful. I remember asking all these questions when I was first separated. Had I been a terrible wife? Was this my fault? What had I done so wrong to be treated this way?

Your brain will try to answer the questions you ask it – just like Google. Notice how most of these questions presuppose a negative answer. They lead you into a negative downward spiral as your brain tries its best to answer them.

This is not what you need right now!

The questions you ask yourself in your mind are vitally important, and the thoughts you have will create goat tracks in your mind. If you've ever walked in the hills, you'll have seen how sheep and goats tend to follow the same path, and over time the paths become clear and established. Your brain is the same – the more you ask the same sort of questions, the stronger the tracks in your mind.

Remember, if you do what you've always done, you'll get what you've always got. So if you find yourself repeatedly in a downward spiral of negative questions, then you need to change what you're doing so that you can get a different result. You always have choice, so choose to do something different.

Use the exercise below to start to think about better questions that you could be asking yourself and choose to ask them instead of the negative spiral questions.

Choose to ask better questions

- On a big piece of paper, write down all the questions that you regularly ask yourself.

- How do those questions make you feel? Do they lead you down a negative spiral, or do they help you to feel better?

- Imagine you can break the power of those negative questions. How will you feel? What will be possible? How differently will you look at what is happening?

- Think of some better questions that you can ask yourself. Some of my favourites are:
  - ➢ What could I do to help myself feel better?

> ➤ What could I do today to show myself that I care about me?
> ➤ Who would be the best person to ask for help with this?
> ➤ What has happened today that was good?
> ➤ What am I grateful for today?
> ➤ What can I do now that I couldn't do before?
> ➤ What is the one tiny upside in all of this?
> ➤ What have I done today that I am proud of?
> ➤ What advice would my best friend give me right now?
> ➤ What one thing always lifts my mood?

- Write them out on post it notes, and stick them up around your house, or keep them by the bed and on the fridge. Perhaps keep a copy in your wallet or bag.

- Next time you find yourself asking a negative spiral question, ask one of your better questions. How do these questions make you feel? What do they lead you to do?

- Notice how they help you to shift your focus away from blame, and towards help and hope. Notice how they shift your focus from the past to the present and future.

By choosing to put your questions where you will see them all the time, you make it more likely that you will remember to ask them when you need them.

Having them in sight all the time helps to create those new goat tracks in your mind.

It may be challenging at first to change your thinking in this way. You will need to make a conscious choice to notice and change your thought patterns. The more you do it, the more you see your questions, and the more you notice how asking them changes the way you are thinking, the more they will become a habitual way of thinking.

Change how you FEEL

Now that you are becoming more aware of how closely your body and mind are connected, and you can shift how you feel very quickly, you can take your ability to shift your feelings even further.

Take a few moments now to ponder:

- Have you ever felt a warm glow of happiness spread through your body?
- Or experienced a heavy feeling of dread when you're anxious?
- Perhaps you feel a red mist rising when you feel angry?
- Does your heart sing or feel so full it will burst when you feel love?
- Maybe you see an image of a beautiful beach or a green forest glade when you feel calm and serene?
- Perhaps your feeling of sadness is heavy and dark, and oval, and it sits in your belly, or maybe it is jagged, sharp and uncomfortable and it sits across your shoulders?

Your feelings will be totally unique to you, and so will be the way in which they show up in your body.

At my lowest moments, I used to feel what I can best describe as a dark "pool of despair" in the pit of my stomach. If I feel afraid, I feel a squirming tangle of nerves in my belly. When I'm excited, I can feel that excitement racing around all my veins like a small racing car.

One client, Jodie, told me that her anger felt like an elephant sitting on her chest. Another said that the anxiety she felt when she thought about facing her ex in mediation was like a tangle of dark blue cables writhing inside her tummy. Another described his fear as a heavy cloak sitting on his shoulders, slowing him down.

Take a few moments to consider how your emotions show up in your body. Do you have an image, or a feeling, or hear a certain sound when you feel a particular feeling? If you could, how would you describe your feelings to me?

The good news is that, however your feelings are showing up in your body, you can shift and change them to reduce the power of your negative feelings so that they are more comfortable, and you can also strengthen and add to the positive feelings.

When you next experience a strong negative emotion, notice how it manifests in your body and mind, and try the exercise below. I suggest reading it through from beginning to end before you start or ask someone to read it out to you bit by bit until you are used to doing it.

Change the physical feeling – Feelings Buster

Next time you experience a strong feeling, take some time to really notice where it is in your body:

- If you knew where the feeling was in your body, where would it be? How would you describe it? What colour would it be? What shape is it? How big is it? Is it moving or is it still? Does it have a weight?

- Is there an image associated with the feeling? Is it black and white or in colour? Is it still or moving? Are you in the picture, or looking at it from a distance? Are the colours sharp or blurred?

- Is there any sound? Is it loud or soft? Is it near or far away? Is the pitch high or low?

Once you have an image or description of how the feeling shows up in your body, you can change it.

- If the feeling has a shape:
    - ➤ change it to a shape that feels more comfortable
    - ➤ change its colour to a colour that you find calming, or that reminds you of your favourite place

---

➢ make it smaller
➢ move it somewhere else in your body –
you could even take it out and throw it
away
➢ if it was moving, slow it down until it is still
➢ change its texture, so that it is smooth
rather than lumpy, or fluffy instead of
sharp
➢ if it moves in one direction, change it so
that it goes the other way

- If the feeling has a picture or image
associated with it:
  ➢ if you feel you are in the scene, imagine
  yourself floating up above the scene,
  seeing it from above
  ➢ imagine yourself floating higher and
  higher, away from the picture
  ➢ make the picture duller and black & white
  ➢ move the image further away from you so
  that it is smaller and dimmer
  ➢ put a frame around the image so that it is
  far away on a screen rather than right in
  front of you

- If the feeling has a sound:
  ➢ change the sound into one you prefer
  ➢ make it quieter and more distant
  ➢ if the sound is low-pitched, make it high;
  if it is high, make it low
  ➢ if the sound is a voice, change it so that
  it sounds silly, or turn it into a song

> ➢ if it is stuck in your mind, sing or shout it out into the air around you, or imagine pulling it out and throwing it into the air to float away.

Using this technique, Jodie changed the elephant sitting on her chest into a soft, fluffy, lilac cushion. She found that her anger now seemed softer and less damaging. It no longer weighed her down.

My other client changed the tangle of dark blue cables of anxiety into orderly yellow strands all neatly tied with a bow, and found she was more able to feel in control of her anxiety when she prepared for mediation. And the third client watched himself take off the heavy cloak of fear that he'd been wearing, and instead saw himself holding a staff of strength and support, given to him by his friends and family.

As for me, I imagine that I have a handful of wonderful fairy dust that I can sprinkle into my pool of despair. The fairy dust fills the pool with sparkly phosphorescence and brightens it up so that doesn't feel so deep and dark anymore.

Let your imagination run free with this exercise. Your emotional brain understands symbols, feelings and images, and when you play with them, you may be surprised by the results!

Notice and enhance your positive emotions too

Just as you can make a conscious choice to notice and change your negative thoughts and feelings, you can also choose to notice and enhance the positive ones.

I remember clearly the first time I felt happy again after my separation. I went to the zoo with my children and some friends and watched a hilarious puppet show (thanks Mr Brown's Pig!). I laughed properly for the first time in 2 months. It was a wonderful moment, when I realised that I would laugh again, and that I could forget about all the stress and worry – even if just for a few minutes.

The Feeling Buster technique isn't only useful to shift negative feelings in your body. You can also use it to enhance positive feelings. You can use it to nurture your positivity.

Enhance the positive emotions using the Feelings Buster technique

Now that you are aware of your feelings, look for times when you feel a positive emotion. When you do something for the first time, notice where that feeling of empowerment and pride is in your body. When you stand tall and feel confident, notice how the feeling manifests in your body and mind.

Go back to the Feelings Buster technique above and use it to strengthen and grow your positive feelings.

Make the feelings bigger, brighter, and more powerful. If you have an associated image, make that image brighter, clearer and crisper. See yourself growing taller and stronger.

Feed and nurture it and help it to grow.

One of my clients found that she had a seed of hope that rested in her chest. She imagined the seed growing every time she felt a positive emotion like pride in an achievement, or when something small made her smile or laugh. The seed of hope over time became a diamond that shone like a beacon in her chest. Another male client felt a tiny orange circle of strength in his heart that he could make bigger and brighter, and he found he could call upon it to help him feel better when he was feeling overwhelmed. Another described her growing confidence as being like a "Readybrek glow" in her body. Once she could visualise and feel it, she was able to call it back so that when she needed to feel confident, she imagined herself glowing from the inside out.

Take each day as it comes. If today was difficult, remind yourself that tomorrow is another day.

In chapter 7, I asked you to create a list of activities that you enjoy, and that take you from stress to soothing. If you haven't already, go back to your list now, so that when you are feeling low you can remind yourself of what makes you happy – and do it. Keep adding to your lists over time, as you discover new things that you enjoy and that make you smile.

These strategies became my go-to techniques whenever something happened during my divorce, to help me manage the intense feelings that arose. They will help you to move from feeling overwhelmed by the immediacy of the feelings, so that you are able to bring calm and bring yourself to a more resourceful place – where you can start to handle whatever is thrown at you with strength and confidence.

In the next chapter, we'll consider how you can build on these techniques, so that you have skills to handle anything your separation might throw your way and take back conscious control of your life.

CHAPTER 10

Taking Back Conscious Control

"If you don't like something, change it. If you can't change it, change your attitude " -Maya Angelou.

Before I go into this chapter, let's take a few moments to look back, and notice what you have already achieved and done.

Todd Herman, better known as the Peak Athlete, coaches professional and Olympic athletes, helping them to increase their performance. He talks about the difference between your "OW brain" and your "WOW brain", and this seems like a great moment to introduce his OW and WOW brain mindset.

Imagine that you are climbing a mountain. You reach the halfway point, and you now have a choice to make. You could a) look up the mountain, and say "OW, look what else I've got left to do". How would that feel? Overwhelming? Impossible?

Or you could look down the mountain, and notice just how far you've come, what you have already done, how you have already changed how you feel and act. You could then look up the mountain with a different approach, and remind yourself that with lots of small steps, you will make it even higher.

Try this for yourself, by consciously choosing to switch your WOW brain on!

Use your WOW brain instead of your OW brain

Think about all the techniques and strategies you have already used from this book, and from any other sources.

Jot down which really made the most difference to you.

Jot down all the things you have done in the last few weeks and months that you couldn't do before, and of which you are proud.

Notice how shifting your focus and understanding your emotions has helped you over the last few days and weeks.

Now that you've got your WOW brain switched on, it's time to look at how you can start to take back conscious control and reclaim power over your life.

To do that, you need to understand what you can and can't control. Often, this conversation leads to a lightbulb moment for people – the moment when they realise that they have been trying to control something that is just not within their power.

What can I control?

How many times have you asked questions like, "Why won't my ex just understand this?", or "I just want to get my ex to listen/stop behaving like that/saying those things"? Or found yourself saying "I have no choice, I just feel so angry"? Maybe you find yourself in a downward spiral when your ex behaves in a way that you just don't understand and feel powerless to change?

I know I asked all those questions and had all those thoughts in the early days. I wanted to make my ex understand my pain, my hurt and my anger. I wanted to control whether/when/how he introduced his new girlfriend to our children. I wanted to make him listen, make him see my point of view, understand and change what he was doing.

Often, we concentrate on trying to control the very things that are most outside our sphere of control. In doing so, we become frustrated, angry, resentful of things that we can't do anything about and have no power over.

This simple diagram illustrates some of the things that you can control, and those which you can't.

The clear zone in the middle is the zone of control – you can control your own stuff. Your own words, actions, thoughts, feelings, behaviours, decisions, body language.

The black zone is where you slip into other people's stuff. You can't control someone else's behaviour or words, or feelings. When you slip into the black zone, the usual result is frustration – because you often don't get the result you want! This is why hoping that you can "make" your ex do something or behave in a certain way is, more often than not, futile.

When you spend your time focusing on how you can get your ex to see your perspective, how you can influence what they are doing, or trying to tell them how to behave, think or respond, you are setting yourself up for failure or at least frustration. You may end up feeling defeated and helpless, exhausted and resentful, angry and embittered. By focusing on your ex and trying to control what they are doing, thinking and saying, you are giving your power away. You are making your peace of mind, your happiness, your mood and state of mind dependent on their actions and behaviours.

Instead, I encourage you to change your focus, shift it to ask yourself what you can do, what you can do to change how you feel and behave. Often, a shift in your approach will result in a shift in theirs. Instead of worrying about what you can't control, shift your energy and focus onto you, what you can control, and what is within your power to do and create.

Remind yourself that it isn't what happens to you that makes the difference. It is what you do with what happens to you.

You might want to print out a copy of the diagram above and stick it up along with all your post-it notes and lists!

At first, you may have to consciously remind yourself of what you can and can't control. You may be stuck in a pattern of trying to control things that are outside your power. If you feel like this, remember if you do what you've always done you'll get what you've always got, so if what you're doing isn't working try anything else.

There are some simple, practical things that you can do right now to take back your power where you can.

Work out where you can take back control, and do it

Your environment

You can control your environment so that you feel safe and comfortable. It is hard to begin to move on and feel better with reminders of the life you are leaving behind surrounding you all the time. Making slight changes can lift your mood, provide concrete satisfaction and give you a sense of achievement and effectiveness. Here are some ideas for making things different.

Make things different

Look around your house and make some changes. Concentrate on one room or area at a time and think about what you could do to make it yours. You could move furniture around, paint a wall, hang new curtains, change the duvet cover. Perhaps buy some new candles, a lamp, or some new cushions.

There might be something you've always wanted to do that your ex didn't - if you have always wanted to paint your bathroom bright turquoise, but they refused, now is your time.

Remove reminders of your old life – so take down those wedding photos, or souvenirs from your honeymoon or last holiday, and replace them with other pictures. Better still, take some new pictures of new memories that you can print and hang. You don't have to get rid of the old pictures, just put them in a box and keep them in storage. If your cushions were wedding presents, and they remind you of memories you'd rather not think of right now, re-cover them or buy some new ones.

You may be surprised at how much a tiny change in your environment can make a huge change to how you feel.

This is, of course, easiest if you are no longer living with your ex. However, even if you are still having to share the same living space, there are things you can do. Is it possible for both of you to have a space that is your safe zone? A space where you know you can retreat and feel comfortable, and that you can make your own? One of my clients had to live with her (very difficult) ex for a few months after their separation. The layout of their house meant that it was tricky to have a room or corner that was just for her, so she created a space in her garden that worked for her. She planted a new border, with beautiful flowers and herbs, and she bought herself a new chair to sit in when she was out there. It became her go-to place, where she felt nourished by the plants she had created and nurtured, and where her ex would never bother her.

Your clothes and appearance

When you're feeling low it can be really tempting not to bother to dress or do your hair or iron your shirt. It might be more comfortable to get dressed every morning in your old tracksuit and bobbly jumper. However, notice how you feel when you do put those clothes on. Do they uplift you, or keep you feeling low?

Much of how we feel is affected by how we dress. When you dress in clothes that help you to feel confident, and that you know look good, notice how it changes how you feel. Would you go to an interview for a new job wearing clothes that made you feel sad and powerless? No! You'd pick the outfit that made you feel confident. Dress to help you feel the way you want to feel.

Dress to feel good

Close your eyes and picture yourself walking out of the house wearing the clothes you normally wear. How are you walking? How are you holding your body? Are you holding your head up high? How are you feeling?

Now picture yourself walking out of the house wearing your favourite clothes, your interview outfit, or the smart clothes you would wear to a party. How are you walking? How are you holding your body? Are you holding your head up high? How are you feeling?

Which outfit is going to help you to feel more positive?

I found it hugely empowering to wear smart clothes and make up when I had to see my ex. I looked more in control, and as a result, I felt more in control. My clothes, and the way I held myself, had a massive effect on how I felt inside.

Who you spend time with

You can control who you spend time with. Go back to your break-up support network and know who you enjoy spending time with, and which are your radiator friends. Remember that you always have choice about accepting or declining invitations – you can turn down invitations from people who leave you feeling drained, or who you know will simply talk about you once you leave.

What you listen to, and watch on TV

The music you listen to, and the programmes you watch on TV can have a big impact on how you feel. So ditch the sad love songs for a while, and listen instead to music that is uplifting, or powerful, and that makes you feel better. If you watch a lot of heavy, depressing drama on TV consider changing to watch programmes that are lighter, more likely to make you laugh. Use your listening and viewing to increase your energy rather than deplete it.

Your routine

You can control your routine, and you can make changes to your routines that help you to feel better and focus on you. Think about how you could shake up your routine.

Shake up your routine

Spend a few moments thinking about all the things you do out of habit. For example, did you and your partner always do certain things in a certain way? Did you have hobbies that you did together? Did you always watch the same kind of programmes on TV? Did you always do the shopping together at the same time, in the same place?

How does doing those things the same way now affect you?

Remember if you do what you've always done, you'll get what you've always got, so if what you're doing isn't working, try anything else!

> If carrying on doing these things make you feel
> miserable, change them or stop doing them. Fill
> the gap with something or someone else.
>
> Jot down some ideas for how you could shake up
> your routine and commit to doing things
> differently.

Perhaps you want to join a new club or group. Try
a new TV series and invite a friend over to watch with
you. Do your shopping on the internet, or on a
different day, and go to a different store. If you always
went for a pint in the same pub on a Friday, choose a
different pub, and buy a different drink.

Likewise, start to notice things that DO work for
you, and do more of them. When you find that doing
your shopping over the internet works really well for
you, keep doing it. When listening to loud pop and
singing along in the car helps you to feel upbeat, do it
more!

Your social media use

You are absolutely in control of your internet use
(although it may not always feel like it!). Resist
subjecting yourself to torture by social media, and the
temptation to check out what your ex is doing on
Facebook/Twitter/Instagram/Snapchat. Defriend,
block, hide. Do not stalk your ex or their new partner
on social media. You don't need to see what they're
doing every day anymore. In fact, you already know
that it's better for you if you can't.

Many of my clients say that their friends tell them
about posts they may have seen on social media. This
is often done with the very best of intentions. Perhaps
they feel aggrieved or angry on your behalf, or they

think it will help you to feel better. I suggest you ask your friends not to tell you about your ex's antics. Explain to them that you don't need to know any more, and that it is in fact better for you if they don't tell you. Ask them to tell you about something else instead. If you find it challenging to ask your friends not to tell you, practice what you want to say beforehand so that you're comfortable with the words you want to use.

Your breathing

You can control your breathing. If you feel overwhelmed or anxious, close the door, sit in a comfortable chair and go back to the "Your breath is more powerful than your thoughts" technique I described in Chapter 7. You could place your hand over your heart as you breathe, to feel it slowing down as you practice this technique.

Your emotions

Have you already been using the techniques earlier in this book to turn down your emotional responses? Notice how you have already taken huge steps towards turning the temperature down and taking back conscious control of your thoughts and feelings, by asking better questions and changing how you feel in the blink of an eye, by trying new things, and shifting your feelings.

Perhaps take a moment to think about which techniques work best for you or go back to read Chapter 9 again!

Your own behaviour

Whilst you can't control your ex's behaviour, you can control your responses to their behaviour. For example, you can refuse to become embroiled in shouting matches, and step away. You can choose to keep your cool. Face-to-face contact has the most potential for conflict, so if you must meet up, plan what you want to say so that you can be clear and specific. Try to keep the conversation positive and end it if you find you aren't making progress. Have a get-away line that you can use to end any conversation calmly but firmly, and practice using it.

Calm behaviour can be contagious! If your interactions with your ex are often argumentative, angry and full of conflict, next time try something different. When you feel your emotional temperature rising, take several deep breaths, and remind yourself that you are always in control of your own behaviour and actions. Do something different and see what different outcome follows.

Use the technique below too, to help you consider your options from another perspective.

Imagine yourself on a stage

Next time you find the emotional temperature rising, take a deep breath, and imagine yourself watching the scene unfold, as if you were watching it happen on a stage in front of you.

How do you feel about the actions you see yourself taking? Do you feel proud? dignified? impressed?

If you were the director of this play, what line would you write in for your character to say, to get a different result?

You could also take a look at Chapter 13, which is packed full of more tips on how to respond rather than react.

Your responses to communication

You can control how you respond to communication. Whenever my ex-husband sent me an angry or upsetting email, I left replying for 24 hours at least. I called this the "24 Hour Rule", and I stuck to it. I learnt the hard way that firing off an equally angry response would only lead to a string of angry emails, and the conflict would escalate, leaving both of us angrier and more frustrated than ever. That wasn't productive or helpful, emotionally or practically. Leaving it for 24 hours gave me time to digest and assess the content of the email, work out what I wanted, and compose a calm and rational response. It gave me time to examine my emotions, work out where they came from, and decide how I wanted to react. It gave me a chance to "sleep on it". Not only that, I could feel that I was the "bigger person", which meant I could feel proud of myself. By doing all this I was maintaining my own boundaries, and he ultimately stopped sending angry and aggressive messages.

I recently worked with a client who used to receive dozens of WhatsApp messages from her ex-partner, often accusing her of all sorts of behaviours over the course of their relationship. She felt that she had to reply to them all to avoid him sending more and more and more. Her replies were usually defensive, and started with words like, "I can't believe that you said ...." and went on to try and justify her position. When we talked about it, I could see the tension and anxiety that this was causing in her. Over the course of our work together she realised that her responses, far from stemming the flow of texts, were encouraging them and feeding the toxic contact that they were having. Once she understood that her responsibility only stretched as far as deciding on her responses, and she wasn't responsible for his beliefs or reactions, she felt much freer to ignore his questions. By taking away the detailed responses that she was giving previously, she was also providing less 'ammunition' for replies. Over time, the messages died away, and the lifting of the tension and anxiety in her body was remarkable.

Now that you have learnt how to feel more in control of your everyday life through making some changes, both practical and emotional, I hope you are noticing that you are better equipped to handle each day with strength and dignity. Now that you've got ideas about how you can take back some control over your environment, and you're taking small steps to take back your power, it's time to think about how you can reframe what is happening to and around you, and build on the brilliant steps you've already taken to move forward positively.

CHAPTER 11

Reframing your Experience

"If you always focus on negative things, you'll feel bad. If you start to look for solutions that are different and better, that's the way your world will become. This is not 'positive thinking', it is brain science." -Richard Bandler

Reframing is one of my favourite techniques. Reframing is all about changing your perspective on a situation, to find something positive or beneficial in it. When you reframe your experience and look at it through a different lens, you can identify unhelpful thoughts and behaviour patterns and replace them with something more positive and hopeful.

Many people find this challenging at first. You may find that you want to resist challenging and changing your thoughts. After all, you are used to thinking in a certain way, and it is comfortable to stay stuck in your negative thoughts. At least you know what they are and where they lead. They may even help you to justify your feeling that you are the victim of circumstance, and someone else is to blame for where you are now. Yes, it is easier to continue down the negative pathways that we have created and practiced over time.

You can train your brain to react differently. If you don't believe me, give the exercises in this chapter a try, just once. Notice what changes and what feels different. When it works, do it again.

It takes a conscious choice to change a negative mindset to a positive one. And it takes practice until you do it without needing to think about it. Over time, and with practice, thinking in a different way will become more natural.

Be grateful for the good things in your life

"Acknowledging the good that you already have in your life is the foundation for all abundance." -Eckhart Tolle

It is incredibly easy not to notice the good stuff when you're on a journey through a separation or divorce. It may feel to you that there is little to be grateful for, and that every day is just hard. There may seem to be little light at the end of the tunnel at times.

Perhaps you are thinking that talking about being grateful is twee or even irritating when life seems very dark. Bear with me – there is scientific evidence to support gratitude as an antidote to negative or challenging emotions.

Consciously shifting your focus from the things that are causing you stress and onto the things that are good in your life starts to re-programme your brain. Imagine that your brain is like a computer, with millions of connections and pathways. The neural pathways that we focus on and use the most often become well used and feel easy. When you focus on what you have lost and you feel sad or angry, that translates into sad or angry thoughts and feelings that can quickly spiral downwards.

What would happen if instead you chose to focus on the good things in your life, even if it was for just a few minutes?

Research has shown that the simple act of writing down things for which you are grateful can have long term benefits such as better sleep, lower stress levels and increased happiness. Being grateful helps the mind to look for the positive, at a time when it may well be more predisposed to see the negative. It can give you a new perspective on your life and help you to see what really matters to you. It has the power to give you hope, to energise and to help you heal.

The evidence shows that people who cultivate being grateful are more immune to stress, be that minor daily hassles or major personal upheavals. They are also more likely to have made progress in moving towards important personal goals, and have better alertness, enthusiasm, determination, attentiveness, resilience and energy. Doesn't that sound good? And doesn't that sound like just what you need right now?

Use this exercise to start noticing the good things:

Choose to notice the good things

Being grateful is a choice, so first set an intention to notice the good things in your life that you might otherwise take for granted.

Record 3-5 things per week for which you are grateful. Make doing this a regular part of your week. You might find last thing at night a good time as it's quiet - and there is the added benefit that you will feel calmer as you lie down to sleep.

Go for depth over breadth – although you can just jot down a couple of sentences, you'll get more out of this practice if you think about why you are grateful, and record that too.

There are all kinds of ways to record the things you are grateful for. Some of the ways that my clients have done this include:

- Keeping a gratitude diary that you use regularly and keep in your bag or by your bed.
- Jotting your thoughts down on paper and keeping them in a gratitude jar. Go back through the posts once a month or whenever you need a boost.
- Creating a visual gratitude board, with pictures and words that you can put up somewhere you can see it whenever you need to.
- Keeping a stack of bright post-it notes around the house, jotting down your thoughts and then sticking them up where you can see them.
- Compiling a Pinterest board of images and quotes.

As I write this, I am grateful that I have just had a cuddle with our puppy, Indy. He is gorgeous and full of joy, bounce, energy and unconditional love for us. I'm also grateful that the sun is shining after a few days of rain, so I don't have to get wet when I walk him. I'm also glad that I spoke to a new friend this morning about meeting up next week, as I like to have things to look forward to. I'm also grateful that my children are happy and flourishing, and that my husband made me a cup of tea this morning.

Being grateful doesn't mean ignoring or stamping on any negative emotions you might be feeling. The practice of finding things that are good helps you to find the positives in your life and ultimately see the opportunities that divorce can bring your way.

Find the upside

You know the old saying, look for the silver lining? Well, it comes in very handy during a break-up. After the initial shock of my separation, I began to realise there were real and significant upsides to my circumstances. I could go for a run when I wanted, without my husband complaining that I'd chosen an inconvenient time. I could eat with the children instead of cooking twice. I could spread out over the whole bed. I didn't have to check with anyone before arranging a night out with friends and I could decide to book a babysitter when I wanted to.

As I started to notice these things, I developed a new way of thinking. Whenever something happened to throw me back to feeling angry or sad or any of my other negative emotions, I challenged myself to find the upside.

I have lost track of how many times over the last decade I have said this to someone who has asked me how I cope with things like being on my own, being a single parent or only having alternate Christmases, and my answer is always the same – there are upsides to divorce; you just have to find them. They range from small to large. For me, the upsides include: I can make my own decisions, I can go on holiday over Christmas every other year if I want to. I have time to pursue my own hobbies and interests in a way that I couldn't before. I can leave the washing up until the morning if I want. I can watch I'm a Celebrity on TV if I choose. I have every other New Year's Eve without my children and can go to a grown-up party. I don't have to freeze on the rugby touchline every Sunday, only every other Sunday!

Try this exercise, to find the upside in your situation.

Find the upside

- If you knew, what is the upside to this?
- What could you do now that you couldn't do before?
- What have you got time for now that you didn't have before?
- What have you learnt from this that will help you in the future?
- If there was a silver lining, what would it be?

When I have asked these questions, I've heard all kinds of answers, ranging from "I can turn the light on when I go to the loo at night now", "We can eat fishfingers and beans when we want", to "I now feel safe in my own home", and "I can make more mess, more noise, and have more fun".

If you try hard enough, you can turn anything on its head.

Tell your story differently

Do you find yourself telling your terrible break-up story repeatedly? Have you noticed that every time you do this, you associate back into all the emotions surrounding it? Have you ever stopped to think about what words you are using to describe your situation? How they make you feel?

Every time you tell the story, you reopen the wounds and keep the emotional ties well and truly alive.

Even now, 12 years on, if I try hard enough I can tell my story in a way that makes me feel sad. If I chose to, I could tell a story of a woman who was left very suddenly one Tuesday night, out of the blue, with no warning, and who found herself overnight catapulted into a world she didn't recognise, feeling abandoned and helpless to influence her future.

Or I can tell a story of a woman who, despite the very sudden and unexpected ending to her marriage, decided she was going to swim not sink, held her head up high, plastered on a smile and over time created a whole new life for her and her children.

Which of those stories sound better to you? Which would you tell if you were me?

You have a choice how to tell your story, so choose to tell it in a way that helps you, empowers you and helps you to feel confident and calm. Use the Rewrite your Story exercise below to help you plan and practice how to tell your story differently.

Rewrite your story

First, notice how you currently tell your story:

- How many times do you tell it in one day?
- What words do you use, and how do they make you feel?
- How do you describe yourself – do you describe yourself as the victim of your divorce?
- How often do you talk about your ex, and the awful things they have done?
- Is your divorce your only topic of conversation?

Notice how people react when you tell the story. Do they feel sorry for you and want to comfort you? Do they try to change the subject, or look to escape as soon as possible? Do they join in with their own stories of terrible relationship breakdowns? All these reactions will also feed the negative emotions attached to your story.

Now think of a different way to tell your story. To tell your story differently, you'll need to ask yourself better questions, for example:

- What have you learnt?
- What are you proud of?
- What have you achieved?
- Have you found any new ways of doing things?

- What have you done that you couldn't do before?
- What different words could you use to describe how you feel?
- How could you shift the focus of your story away from your ex?

Create a list of all the things you have done that you are proud of, and that you couldn't do before, and talk about those instead of telling the terrible, sad story. Instead of telling people how badly you have been treated, start to tell them how you have been able to do and learn new things.

Now that you have a new story prepared, try it out:

- How does it feel to you to tell this new story?
- How do you feel inside when you tell it?
- When you tell it to other people, how do they react differently?

I found that people's reactions to me and my story changed dramatically once I started telling my story differently. Instead of feeling they had to commiserate with me, or be angry on my behalf, people started telling me what an amazing job I was doing, how brilliantly they thought I was handling things, and how impressed they were by my attitude. As a side effect of telling a different story, I found I was also getting a much more positive and empowering reaction from the people I was talking to. Instead of being caught in a downward spiral, I now found myself on an upward one, one that was much more uplifting and hopeful.

Ultimately, it's your attitude that will make the difference and enable you to move forward through your divorce and beyond. You have the power to choose to use these techniques to consciously create new and better ways of thinking, which will change the way you feel and act.

In the next chapter, we'll look at strategies to face the things that you are afraid of, and how to minimise the uncertainty that you might be feeling right now.

CHAPTER 12

Facing your Fears

"There are four ways you can handle fear. You can go over it, under it, or around it. But if you are ever to put fear behind you, you must walk straight through it" -Donna Favors

You've taken steps now to start to reclaim your life and taken back control where you can by shifting your focus on to you and turning down the volume on your challenging emotions. Now it's time to look at those things that you are afraid of. When you are in a state of transition and change, and you feel like your life has been turned upside down, it is normal to feel scared and unsure. After all, the future is unknown and uncertain right now.

Your brain is hardwired to react to uncertainty with fear – it's an automatic, primitive reaction that prepares the body to for "fight or flight" in response to a perceived harmful event, attack or threat to survival. When faced with an imminent danger, like a growling dog or a runaway train racing towards you, fear is useful as it stimulates our fight or flight response. It causes release of adrenalin and cortisol and enables you to react quickly to the danger without needing to stop and think first. Once the danger has passed, the adrenalin and cortisol reduce, and normality can return.

This automatic response is not so useful when you are not afraid of an immediate danger, but of an uncertain future. That fear can distort your thinking and make you feel anxious on an ongoing basis. Fear and anxiety can become the lens through which you see the world, meaning that you are in a constant state of high stress and arousal. It can keep you trapped, unable to move forward – and this is why it is so important to face your fears.

Sometimes, fear can mean that of our coping mechanisms fly out of the window, as the emotional brain takes over. Remember that you know lots of different techniques to help you handle your fear. Many of the techniques you have learnt earlier in this book will help you now. Breathing through your stress responses and using the techniques to reduce the temperature on your emotions will help you to feel calmer. Remember that you already know how to change how you feel in the blink of an eye, and you've got your better questions stuck up around your house on post-it notes. You have strategies to change the physical feelings, and you know how to stand to increase your confidence. You have all the resources you need!

What can you then do to handle your fears and minimise the uncertainty that you are facing? The good news is that you can change the filter, and your future is in your hands.

Facing your fears

The first thing I want to do is tell you a story. This is a Buddhist story that I first read in Pema Chodron's book 'When things fall apart – heart advice for difficult times', and it is a beautiful illustration of how powerful it is to face your fears head on:

"Once there was a young warrior. Her teacher told her that she had to do battle with fear. She didn't want to do that. It seemed too aggressive; it was scary; it seemed unfriendly. But the teacher said she had to do it and gave her the instructions for the battle.

The day arrived. The student warrior stood on one side, and fear stood on the other. The warrior was feeling very small, and fear was looking big and wrathful. They both had their weapons. The young warrior roused herself and went towards fear, prostrated three times and asked, 'May I have permission to go into battle with you?'

Fear said 'Thank you for showing me so much respect that you ask permission.' Then the young warrior said, 'How can I defeat you?'.

Fear replied, 'My weapons are that I talk fast, and I get very close to your face. Then you get completely unnerved, and you do whatever I say. If you don't do what I tell you, I have no power. You can listen to me, and you can have respect for me. You can even be convinced by me. But if you don't do what I say, I have no power.'

In that way, the student warrior learned how to defeat fear."

This wonderfully simple story shows that fear might be there to warn you, that it can be intimidating and scary but ultimately if you don't do what it says it has no hold over you.

When you face a fear head on it reduces its power over you. When you avoid or give in to a fear, you increase its hold over you and you give your power away.

Get clarity around the things that scare you

Some of your fear might arise from lack of knowledge or fear of the unknown, and it helps to get clarity around those fears. The unknown is scary because you don't know what it will look like and your imagination may start to create all kinds of "what if's" around how it could look.

It is always better to know where you are rather than live in the shadow of "what if". I often describe a "what-if-tree" to my clients. Imagine each "what if" scenario as a branch on your very own what-if-tree. Every time you worry about all the what if's, you feed and nurture the what-if-tree so that it grows and casts a long shadow. Every time you face one of your fears, or what if scenarios, imagine yourself cutting a branch off the what-if-tree, the shadow becomes lighter and the sun can shine through. Imagine what it would feel like to get rid of that tree completely!

The starting point is to brainstorm your fears and start to think of small steps you can take to get clarity and move through them, one at a time.

Brainstorm your fears

Brainstorm all your worries and fears on a big piece of paper. Take your time doing this and write down anything that comes to mind.

How do those fears and worries make you feel? Jot down any feelings that come to mind. Allow yourself to sit with the feelings for a couple of minutes and notice how they feel in your body. Identify them and acknowledge them.

If those feelings conjure up a feeling in your body, or an image in your mind, you could take a pause to use the Feelings Buster to turn down the temperature on those feelings, so that they are more comfortable.

Notice where your fears and worries and the emotions surrounding them lead your thoughts. Perhaps your mind starts to go off in all directions? Perhaps you find yourself in a downward spiral of internal questions?

Imagine what it would feel to be free of the fears and worries. Imagine you could rub them all out, erase them, and have a clean page free of fear and worry. Or imagine you could screw them all up and throw them away.

- How would you feel then?
- What would life be like?
- What would you see and hear around you if you could get rid of that fear?
- What would become possible?

Now ask yourself better questions. For example:

- What do I need to find out about to get clarity around the things I fear?
- What small steps can I take to reduce this fear?
- What skills do I have that could help me right now?
- Have I ever dealt with anything like this before? What exactly did I do?
- What strengths or qualities have I used in the past that could help me now?
- Who can I ask for advice around this?
- Who do I know who has done this well?
- What choices and options do I have (find at least 3)
- What would my best friend advise me to do right now?

What three things could you do right now, today, to get more clarity and start to move through your fears and worries so that you can focus on taking positive steps forward with confidence and certainty.

Write out your three things and commit to doing them!

You could screw up, shred, or even burn your original brainstorm to symbolically let go of those fears.

When you have more clarity, you diminish the "what if" possibilities and arm yourself with information and knowledge. This will reduce the overwhelm that comes with the unknown.

For example, if your future financial position is uncertain and worrying you, work out your income and budget or ask a financial adviser to help you. Even if the picture is not as you would wish, at least you are no longer in the scary position of not knowing. Once you are aware of any shortfall you can work with the facts, not the "what if's" and start to plan how you could fill the gap or change and prioritise your spending.

Or, if you are scared by the prospect of spending weekends on your own while your children are with their other parent, ask yourself who you know who deals with this well. Talk to them and ask them how they spend their time when the children are away. Ask further better questions, for example:

- Is there something you have always wanted to do, but never had the time?
- Is there a hobby you have always wanted to try?
- Do you have friends you don't see often because they're too far away? Could you arrange to visit them during one of your weekends?
- What can you do now that wasn't possible before?

Make a conscious decision to make the best of the situation. Be in control of it, rather than letting it control you.

Remember to use your WOW brain

In Chapter 10, I introduced you to Todd Herman's concept of the OW and WOW brains. This can be a really good tool to use to reframe where you are right now and where you want to be. By using your WOW brain, you can remind yourself of all the amazing things you have already done and learnt. By noticing what you have already achieved, you remind yourself of just how resourceful you are.

I remember the first time I mowed the lawn after my ex-husband left. I had put it off for weeks, but finally I did it, and I felt proud. To put this into context, this wasn't a small patch of grass but a 100 feet stretch of not-very-well-looked-after grass on a slope with wonky borders and plenty of small plastic toys left from the boys' playing. It sounds like a small thing, but it is one of my clearest memories from that time.

Use this exercise to use your WOW brain to help you face your fears and access your resourcefulness.

Using your WOW brain to face your fears

Take a few moments to think about these questions:

- What have you done in the last week/month/year that you couldn't do before?
- What can you learn from this, so that you can do it better tomorrow?
- What have you achieved that you are proud of?

- How did you feel when you achieved that?
- What have you overcome in the last month/2 months/year?

Create a "WOW list" of all the things you have achieved, and all the times you have faced something that scared you.

Keep your list somewhere you can see it easily and remind yourself of your achievements whenever you start to question yourself. You could also turn some of your achievements into affirmations, to remind yourself of how far you have travelled.

Visualise your fears in a different way

The imagination and memory fire the same circuits in the brain, so when you use your imagination to visualise your fears in a different way, it can be very powerful.

How do your fears show up in your body and mind?

One of my clients always felt her fears as a pool in her belly. The pool was dark and deep and scary and she imagined herself standing on the rocks to the side feeling apprehensive and afraid. In one of our sessions we talked about her fear of organising her finances. After looking at all the other things she had achieved over the last 6 months, she saw that being in sole charge of her bank account was not so scary after all. Her perspective started to shift as she looked through the lens of what she had already learned and achieved.

We talked about the resources she would need including who she could ask for help and she imagined herself putting those resources into her Worry Pool. Eventually she felt strong enough to imagine herself diving in.

Before our next session, she had gone through her financial information, opened a new bank account and transferred her payments across to the new account. Once she had done this, she knew that she could do things that at first seemed impossible and scary. The pool no longer seemed so dark or deep and it contained resources that she could use again and again. Every time she imagined herself diving into the pool, she emerged stronger and more confident than before.

Remember that every time you face one of your fears, you increase the clarity you have around your situation. By facing your fears, you are consciously taking back control of your life, your decisions and your future – because you are not letting them be controlled by fear. You are not letting your fears define you.

I know how daunting it can be to face your fears head on. Notice that every time you do something new, or learn something, or do something despite your fear, you are growing stronger and stronger. Like the warrior in the story, you are being courageous and brave. You might have looked at some really scary stuff over this chapter, and I want you to notice just how far you've come since you started your journey. Even if you took one small step towards doing something new or different, or something that scared you, stop to notice. It is so important to notice when you overcome a fear or do something despite feeling afraid. Feel proud, stand tall and know that you can do this. Keep writing your achievements down in your journal so that you can look back when you need to and remind yourself of just how much you can do.

Many of my clients say that one of their biggest fears is they won't know how to respond when something happens that is unexpected or out of the blue. So let's take a look at some techniques you can use to respond rather than react.

CHAPTER 13

Responding Rather than Reacting

"Everything can be taken from a man but one thing: the last of the human freedoms—to choose one's attitude in any given set of circumstances, to choose one's own way" -Viktor Frankl

In this chapter, we'll start to look at how you can use the techniques and strategies you've already gained to help you respond rather than react to the curveballs that separation and divorce can throw your way. These techniques will help you to communicate more successfully with your ex, and to keep your cool when your divorce throws an unexpected curveball.

When something happens, and your emotional temperature rises, several things happen. Your emotions will start to influence your thoughts and your body. Perhaps you start to sweat, your head feels cloudy, your heart and breathing rates increase, your stomach clenches or knots itself up. At the same time, thoughts will probably start to swirl around your head. These might include thoughts like:

- It's so unfair
- I don't deserve this
- He/she is such a ****
- Nothing ever changes, so what's the point – this will never get any better
- I must be a bad person
- I can't do this any more
- I feel totally alone
- What if ....

The combination of rising emotion, fear, physical reaction and spiralling thoughts can lead you to react very quickly and instinctively, without thinking. I've been there too. In Chapter 8, I told you about the time I shouted obscenities at my ex-husband in the street, while he stood and watched quietly. He had said something that triggered the threat response in my brain, and BOOM! I went straight into "fight" mode without hesitating.

Remember that the fight, flight or freeze response to stress is completely normal. When your emotional brain floods the logical brain, your instinctive reaction is to fight, or run away, or freeze.

There is also a less-often mentioned fourth response – the "fawn response". This is when your response is to try and please another person, in order to avoid conflict. You may find yourself monitoring the other person's state of mind, to anticipate what they might do or feel, and adapting your responses to minimise confrontation.

In a divorce situation, a fight reaction might result in arguing, shouting, threatening. A flight reaction might mean you withdraw, walk away from any discussion or throw in the towel and give up. A freeze reaction might mean you ignore correspondence or information, hoping that it will all go away. A fawn response would see you adapting your behaviour in order to appease or please.

None of these reactions will help in the long run. They might make you feel better for a short while, but eventually, they will come back to haunt you. I know that shouting at my ex in the street made me feel better for a few moments, but then I felt ashamed and embarrassed. That didn't help.

By contrast, the times that I was able to respond calmly and with dignity meant that my sense of pride in myself grew. When you can take the emotion out of your communication, and respond rather than react, you are doing yourself a huge favour, and probably saving yourself thousands in legal fees.

What could I have done differently in that moment of heightened emotional reaction?

Stop. Breathe. Think. Act.

This mantra was incredibly useful for me during my divorce. You already know how to stop and breathe to take power back over your swirling thoughts, and that technique will come in handy whenever you feel your emotions leading your reactions.

When you stop to remind yourself to breathe, you give yourself space. The oxygen that you breathe in helps to calm the emotional responses in your brain, slow your heartrate, and reduce the stress response.

Scientists have now found evidence to show the power of breathing to calm emotional responses. By breathing deeply, you can change your emotional state and ability to react differently. Your breath has the power to overcome the immediate stress response that might otherwise cause you to act without thinking.

The oxygen that you breathe into your body calms the emotional part of the brain. Simply stopping to take three deep breaths before you respond is a great start. You could also use the "Your breath is more powerful than your thoughts" exercise in Chapter 7 to focus on your breath rather than on your swirling thoughts, and the stress response will reduce.

Once you are aware of your emotional reaction rising, breathing is always the first step. Once you have used your breath to bring calm and interrupt the swirling thoughts, then you have bought yourself time to think, and consider your choices before you act.

Give yourself a reminder to stop and breathe

Perhaps you are thinking "But when that reaction comes, I don't have time to stop and breathe!", or "But how will I remember to stop, the feelings are just too strong!". Perhaps you feel that the emotional reactions you have are unstoppable, uncontrollable. You "see red" and act instinctively – how can you control that?

I promise you that you can. The first time will always be the hardest. Every time you do it, the easier it will become. Ultimately, who has power over your brain? YOU DO! You have the power to change your reactions. In fact, when you think you can only react in one way to something external – the situation, your ex, your email inbox – you give away your power. When you tell yourself that you can't do it, guess what, you're right! When you tell yourself that you CAN, what shifts? Notice how differently you feel.

"You will continue to suffer if you have an emotional reaction to everything that is said to you. If words control you, that means everyone else can control you. Breathe and allow things to pass!"
-Warren Buffet

Once you start to be more aware of your emotions rising, you might find it helpful to have a physical reminder of your ability to stop and breathe. The exercise below is designed to help you consider how you could remind yourself and notice how much difference it could make to your reactions and responses.

Stop, breathe, think, act

Think back over the last few weeks – have there been times when this mantra could have helped you?

Make a list of any occasions when your emotions overwhelmed you, and you reacted instinctively.

What difference would it have made if you had stopped to breathe before responding?

Take a moment to consider how you could start to bring in a "stop, breathe, think, act" response to rising emotions. Some of the ideas I have used with clients are below:

- Keep an elastic band around your wrist to ping when you feel the emotions rising
- Create a signal to remind you to stop and breathe, like pressing your thumb and forefinger together
- Repeat "Stop, breathe, think act!" to yourself
- Put post it notes up around your home with the words on to remind you
- Find a piece of music that you can bring to mind to help you remember

Next time you feel the emotions rising, notice how much difference it makes when you stop, breathe and think before you act.

After stopping and breathing, then it's time to really take back your power, and look at your choices.

Remember if you keep doing the same thing, and getting the same result that isn't working, choose anything else!

Choice is better than no choice - choosing your emotional responses

I always say to clients that choice is better than no choice. When you feel you only have one option, you are stuck. When you have two options, you face a dilemma. When you have three or more options, you have choice. It is choice that matters, and seeing choices gives you power to make a conscious decision to follow one route or another.

You always have a choice how to respond. Let's look again at the time I shouted at my ex-husband in the street. In that moment, what were my choices? These are the five that come to mind immediately:

- Shout and scream at him
- Cry and storm off
- Breathe and tell him that what he had just said hurt me
- Breathe and let him know I was walking away from being spoken to disrespectfully
- Breathe and calmly say that I would speak to him another time

Try this exercise to think about your choices in responding differently.

Choice is better than no choice

Take a few moments now to think about how you might have reacted in my situation. Are there other choices that you can see?

Now go back to the times you listed when "Stop, breathe, think, act" would have helped you to respond differently. Write down at least 3 different options for how you could have responded on each occasion.

How could using any of those options have led to a better outcome for you?

Which options will you try next time?

The mantra of 'choice is better than no choice' has kept me sane on many an occasion. In order to think of at least 3 choices, I have to stop, breathe and think. It stops my emotional brain from taking over, and brings my logical, rational brain back into the game.

Of course, you'll have moments where you act out of sheer emotional frustration. When that happens, take stock, recognise what happened, and be kind to yourself. Forgive yourself. Think about how you might better respond the next time you feel that way. Remind yourself that choice is better than no choice, and that you always have a choice about how you react to any situation. How could you do it better next time? What different choice could you have made?

Notice when you do well and notice what works. Every time you remember to stop, breathe, think, act, and you choose to react more constructively, feel proud, and give yourself a big pat on the back. It will get easier every time.

When I first met with my client, Jodie, she was angry that her ex-husband had left many of his possessions in the house. He had moved out and was living in a different property. We talked about her choices, and she saw that she could:

- Ask him to come and collect them
- Put it all in the loft or the garage
- Leave it where it was
- Box it up and give it to him in stages
- Sell it at a car boot sale

She chose to start editing all his things, sort them into boxes, and ask him to collect them. This of course left him with a choice as to whether to collect them or not. She decided that if he refused, then she would store it all in boxes in the loft – out of sight, out of mind.

Take control of your side of written communication

If there are certain triggers for your strong feelings, think in advance about what you can do to take back your power in the situation. What are your choices and options?

Emails, texts and communication from your ex are often trigger points, so have a plan for how you will respond, starting with Stop, Breathe, Think, Act. As we saw in Chapter 10, you have the power to take back control over your responses to communication.

In the early days of my divorce, I found almost every email that my ex sent upsetting. Just seeing his name in my inbox meant that I felt stressed and anxious, and I know that many of my clients feel this way too. It reminded me how out of control I felt in the situation I found myself in, and I felt scared. I decided that I needed to take some control back.

I noticed that responding immediately and aggressively made me feel worse, as I would then dread the inevitable angry reply.

Remember the "24 Hour Rule" I mentioned in Chapter 10? This was my rule that I would not reply to any message or email that made me angry for at least 24 hours. It gave me time to take stock, acknowledge how I felt, and consider what sort of response would work best for me. It gave me time to choose. It meant that whenever an email from him pinged into my inbox, I knew I had time. It also meant that we didn't get trapped in increasingly emotional and argumentative exchanges that would fan the flames.

By taking control of your choices and your behaviour in this way, you will feel empowered, more confident and calmer.

One of my clients recently took the 24 Hour Rule even further. Her ex was particularly challenging, and he sent her numerous messages every day, at all sorts of times, often when she was with their son. She felt hounded, permanently on edge, and powerless to change the situation. We talked about choices and came up with a list of possible options to consider.

She took these decisions:

- Buy a new phone and keep only her ex's number on her old one.
- Set up a new email account and ask all her friends to use it, keeping her old one for her ex only.
- Check each account twice a day at certain times when she was able to look properly, and never just before bed.
- Forward any particularly nasty or angry messages to a friend, who would read them and pick out the points that needed answering.
- Reply to all the messages in one reply, including responses to the points that mattered, and nothing else.

As a result of these choices, random messages no longer pinged into her inbox, interrupting time with their child, or causing her to panic. She found that she was no longer anxiously awaiting a ping from her phone. Her feeling of being in control increased and she realised she wasn't powerless. Instead, she now felt safe from the previously constant messages from her ex.

After a few weeks, her new way of dealing with the messages meant that not only did the number of messages her ex was sending decline, but they also became more polite and less angry. She felt more confident, more empowered and stronger to respond in an effective way.

Know that you can ask better questions

Remember all those questions you used to help turn down the temperature on your feelings? Those too will be important right now, to break the cycle of swirling questions in your mind. Interrupt the swirling questions and replace them with questions that will take you forward, that will help you think about your choices. Some really good ones might be:

- What choices do I have right now?
- What would be the right thing to do?
- What would I do right now if I was being my best self?

Create your own list of the questions that you find most helpful and keep it where you can easily access it should you need to.

When you combine your ability to respond rather than react with all the other skills you now have of finding the upside, looking for the good, and taking back power over your mind and your thoughts, notice what a truly impressive set of tools you have to handle anything that may come your way!

With strategies up your sleeve for taking back your power over your emotional responses, the next chapter will look at that thorny subject –

communicating with your ex. When you're feeling hurt or abandoned, or angry, it can be tempting to take all that emotion into any meetings with your ex. You know I'm going to say that this will backfire. It may make your divorce way more challenging, painful and expensive than it needs to be. I'm going to share with you some ways in which you can take the lead, and communicate more successfully with your ex.

CHAPTER 14

Communication Tips

One of the most challenging aspects of divorce for many of my clients is communication with their ex. The person you used to share everything with is suddenly cast in a different role, and you may find yourself in a cycle of conflict, recriminations, and "you always", "you never" kind of conversations that only ever lead to anger and defensiveness. Emotions are running high, and you may both be approaching your communication from a place of fear and uncertainty.

It is easy for me to say that the best way forward is to take the emotion out of your communication. How can you achieve this? What if your ex is aggressive, or angry, or never lets you speak? What if they refuse to speak at all, or just don't respond to any correspondence from you?

Well, remember that you already have lots of techniques to take back your power over your reactions. You have learnt to breathe to calm your emotional brain, and you know how to turn down the temperature on your strong emotions. These techniques will be invaluable when it comes to communication with your ex.

The strategies I outline below will help you to stay in control of your own reactions and responses, and take the lead, even if your ex is not co-operative.

Know your intentions

Although you might feel very strongly now, it is important to know what you want your relationship with your ex to look like in the future, and to consider how you want to feel about your part in it as time goes by.

Use this exercise to start to get clear on your vision for your relationship in the future.

Your vision for your future relationship

Take a fresh page in your diary, and jot down anything that comes to mind as you contemplate these questions:

- What do you want your relationship to look like in 1 year?
- In 5 years?
- In 10 years?
- At your child's wedding?
- How do you want to feel when you look back at what you do and say now?

Doing this exercise can help to bring your goals into focus. I knew, for example, that I wanted our children to feel free to have a positive relationship with both of us, and I knew that when the time came for weddings/graduations/21st birthday parties, I did not want them to worry about whether their dad and I could be in the same room together. Instead, I wanted them not just to know that there would not be a problem, but for it not even to be a consideration for them in their planning. I wanted to have a civil, respectful relationship with my ex-husband and his partner (now his wife), and I wanted to feel proud that I was setting a great example for our children.

Your vision might be different. If your ex is challenging, perhaps your goal is simply to be able to communicate briefly with them about arrangements in a respectful way and nothing more. Perhaps it is to be able to exit the relationship without bitterness and then never see each other again, especially if you do not have children.

Whatever your vision is, keep it in the forefront of your mind. Every time you communicate with your ex, remind yourself of the long-term vision, and ask yourself whether your words or actions will take you further towards or away from that vision.

Communicate your intentions

You may find it helpful to communicate your intentions to your ex. I told my ex-husband that my intention was to do the very best for our children throughout, and that it was important to me that we were able to be civil and polite. You may find, like me, that your ex has the same intention. If that's the case, then you have a great common ground from which to start. If not, then keep your intention safe, act in accordance with it, and you may be surprised at how things shift over time.

Be honest with yourself about your intentions

It's also important to be totally honest with yourself about your intentions. If, deep down your intention really is to punish your ex, or to make their life as difficult as possible, or to hurt them in the same way that they have hurt you, first acknowledge that intention. Then ask yourself whether having that intention is really serving you. Is it the right thing to do? Is it keeping you stuck in conflict or pain? What might be a better intention to hold?

I remember the sudden lightbulb moment when I realised that staying angry with my ex was only going to damage me. It was keeping me stuck in negative thoughts and feelings, and it was contributing to my feelings of depression. And it was hard work! Being angry requires using energy that I realised could be better spent focusing on me and my life. Now, I often say to clients that holding onto anger is like drinking poison and expecting someone else to die. Anger can feel like an unwelcome lodger in your head. It can eat you up and take away your future. Don't let your anger define you. Instead, remind yourself that YOU define you. You can choose who you become.

Remember what you can and can't control

As you already know from Chapter 10, you can only control your own actions, words, choices and behaviours. Whilst you are, of course, free to put across your opinion and perspective, your ex also has a choice about how they respond.

If your way of communicating is resulting in increased conflict and stress for you, what could you do differently? If you do what you've always done, you'll get what you've always got, so if what you're doing isn't working, try anything else!

When I shouted at my ex or used sentences that began with "you never", or "you always", the result was inevitably an increase in defensiveness, anger or frustration – on both our parts. I used my mantra of "dignity at all times", along with my vision of our future relationship to motivate me to try other techniques. Sometimes it meant biting my tongue or using the 24 Hour Rule to stop myself from firing off an angry text or email. In the grand scheme of things, and over a decade later, I am so glad that I did.

Use the Stop, Breathe, Think, Act strategy

You already know the Stop, Breathe, Think, Act technique, and use it to respond rather than react. It only takes a few seconds to practice, and can make all the difference when you feel the emotional temperature rising during communication with your ex. Taking those few seconds to pause and think can have a huge effect on your ability to respond calmly and logically.

You could also use the "Your breath is more powerful than your thoughts" exercise from Chapter 7 to help you take back power over your thoughts. Use your breath to shift your focus away from the thoughts and feelings in your head, quieting your mind and reducing the stress response.

Sleep on it

Have you ever noticed how a night's sleep can change how you feel when you wake up? When you sleep, your conscious mind switches off and your subconscious has time to process everything that has happened and is happening to you. It stores all your memories and uses your rest time to process your emotions. It often comes up with new ways of approaching something.

"Sleep on it" is an old cliché, but as ever there is truth behind the words!

Many of my clients find that the sight of their ex's name popping up in their inbox or on their phone sets of their stress response. Once you have calmed your reaction using your breath, remind yourself that most correspondence does not require an immediate response. Use the 24 Hour Rule to avoid replying while you are angry or upset. Sleep on it. You may be surprised by the difference a night's sleep can make to how you feel, how you interpret their message and what you want to say.

Notice and challenge your assumptions

An assumption is something that you accept as true without questioning it, and without seeking proof. As a result, you don't ask for clarification. Instead, you accept it, believe it and act in accordance with it.

This doesn't always help when you are trying to negotiate or communicate with your ex during a break-up. I know that when I was going through my divorce, I found myself thinking "He's only doing that to wind me up" on many occasions.

I worked with my client, Caroline, around this very recently. Her ex was not responding to any letters from her lawyer and Caroline saw this as him being contemptuous towards her. She said that it made her feel worthless and as though she didn't even exist. She felt depressed and tearful as a result and her confidence took a big knock. She assumed that her ex was behaving in this way because he had no respect for her, that she was nothing to him.

When I asked Caroline whether she was 100% sure that this was his motivation, she hesitated. I asked her what else his intentions could be. After a few moments, she said that it could be that he was frightened of the process; after all there was a lot at stake in their negotiations. Perhaps he was burying his head in the sand, rather than deliberately showing contempt for her. Perhaps he was scared. Perhaps he was responding to his stress by going into flight and pretending this wasn't happening.

Once Caroline had challenged her own assumption, she saw that she was allowing his lack of response to dictate how she felt. She was allowing his actions to control her feelings, and she was becoming angry and frustrated because she could not change his behaviour. Once she had realised this, it opened the door for us to examine what Caroline could do to change how she felt, and how she saw her ex's lack of responses.

I asked her to tell me about some of the things she had achieved over the last 6 months, and to tell me about some of the good things in her life. As she talked, she started to see how resourceful she was and how much she had achieved since their split. She started to wonder if her ex's lack of response was actually because he could see how strong and resourceful she had become! She wrote some great mantras on post-it notes to take home and stick up to remind herself:

- I choose how I feel
- I am strong and resourceful
- I can handle this

By challenging her immediate assumptions, Caroline was able to see that she could turn her feelings around and be 100% certain that she could hold her head up high.

Try this exercise, to challenge any assumptions that you might be making.

Challenge your assumptions

Do you assume you know why your ex is behaving in a certain way? That they are only "doing that to hurt me", or "punish me"?

Think back to the last time that this happened. What was happening? How did you feel, and what did you assume about your ex's words or actions?

- Are you 100% sure that you are right?
- What else could their intention be?
- What feelings might be behind their actions or words?

Sometimes, it is important to remember that they too are going through this break-up, and they too will be responding out of fear and hurt at times.

Take a helicopter view

When emotions are running high, it's easy to get lost in the feelings and say things you regret later.

I often use the technique below with clients to help them think through their feelings and emotions around some of the more "thorny" discussion points with their ex.

Take a Helicopter View

Think of an issue that you and your ex have fallen out about recently.

Stand or sit in a chair and explain out loud, or by writing it down, what your perspective on it is:

- What do you see, hear and feel?
- What do you believe?
- How do you see it?

Once you've done that, shake your body off. Really shake it off – shake your arms, legs and body.

Move to a different space or chair. Imagine that you are your ex. You have your ex's history, experiences, beliefs and outlook. Really feel into what it is like to be them facing this particular issue. Now explain out loud, or by writing it down, what their perspective is.

Use "I" to do this – remember you are doing this as though you are your ex, from their perspective:

- What do you see, hear and feel?
- What do you believe?
- How do you see it?

Again, shake your body off.

Take a step back and imagine that you are looking at you and your ex from the perspective of an independent third person – someone who has no strong feelings about the issue, and who is supportive of you both.

They have a good view of you both and can see and hear you both:

- What does that person notice about you and your ex in this situation?
- What message or advice might they give you both?

Go back over your answers. What do you notice about how you, your ex and the independent third party see and feel? What did you learn? How could you use this information going forward?

I recently did this exercise with a client who had been through a long, expensive court process, which had not ended with the result she had wanted. As we talked through the different perspectives, she realised that both she and her ex had become caught up in their own positions so much that neither had even considered there could be a different viewpoint. Not only this, they had both forgotten all about the children who were caught in the middle.

She remarked afterwards that she wished she had come to see me two years earlier, as it could have made a huge difference to both the legal costs and outcome of their divorce.

Listen to understand, rather than to respond

Real listening is a great skill and is hugely valuable right now. Often as we 'listen', what we are really doing is thinking about what we're going to say next – which means we aren't really listening at all. It means that you can miss important messages. Your brain is busy responding emotionally and putting up defences or preparing your next attack. This will only escalate conflict and is where discussions often collapse into point-scoring.

Breathing can help again here. While your ex is talking, concentrate on listening. Listen out for which words they are using, and clues as to their intentions. If you are unsure about anything, ask.Ask them to explain why something is so important to them. A great parenting coach I work with, Mette Theilmann, has a great mantra for this – "Be curious, not furious".

Speak from the "I"

Avoid sentences that start with "you always" or "you never", as these are pretty much guaranteed to lead you further into a cycle of conflict and blame. Instead, focus on expressing your own feelings and needs.

"I felt angry when I heard you say that" is far less judgmental than "You make me feel angry", as it isn't blaming or shaming the other person, and it isn't trying to make them responsible for your feelings.

Try this formula:

I feel .... when ...., so I would like it if/could we try/would you be able to ....

A couple of examples:

- I feel frustrated when I don't think I'm being heard, so perhaps we could speak in turns for 3 minutes each.
- I feel afraid when you raise your voice, as I want to work towards a calm resolution of this issue, so I would like it if you could speak in a quiet voice.

- I feel angry when I hear you say that because I need to feel respected and I hear your words as an insult, so would you be able to tell me what you need instead of what you think of me?

Speak firmly and clearly and make your request a positive one.

Once you have made a request, your ex then has a choice of response. They may refuse to do what you ask, and you then have a choice as to whether you continue with the conversation.

This sort of communication technique can work wonders when you are accidentally hurting each other, but there are times when it may be better to put a firm boundary in place, such as "when you shout at me I feel angry and I am not willing to be shouted at, so I am leaving now".

Be aware of your body language

Did you know that only 7% of what we communicate is in the actual words we use? The other 93% is non-verbal - the tone of voice you use (38%) and body language (55%).

Research shows that when the words we use and the non-verbal signals we give don't match, people believe the non-verbal every time. Ever had someone say "sorry" to you, whilst they roll their eyes and use a sarcastic tone? Me too! They weren't really sorry at all, were they?

So be aware of your tone and body language.

Be the Steven Spielberg of your own mind

Controlling your reactions to written communication is one thing. Preparing to see your ex in person, attending a mediation session or court hearing is something else again. Perhaps you feel anxious about seeing your ex again, or you are dreading sitting across a table from him/her in mediation or in court. I remember my nerves and the sicky feeling in my stomach before my first round-table meeting with my ex and our lawyers.

The better prepared you are emotionally for these meetings, the better you will feel about them.

Your mind doesn't know the difference between what you imagine and what you remember – the memory and the imagination fire the same circuits in your brain. You can use this knowledge to decrease your fear of these scenarios by becoming the Steven Spielberg of your own mind. Many actors and sports performers use this technique to help them improve and maintain their performance, and you can too.

One of my clients was afraid of bumping into her ex on public transport in London, a fear that was causing her to feel anxious. We used the technique below to practice how she would sit on the Tube, how she would look at her ex, and what line she could use to exit the conversation.

Another client used it to prepare for her first mediation meeting with her ex. Before she went to the meeting, she knew how she would walk into the room, what she would be wearing, and how she would speak. She also knew how she would walk away, should that prove necessary. As a result, her anxiety decreased, as she felt so much more certain as to what she was going to do and say in the meeting, and she was no longer afraid that she would simply cry or find it impossible to speak at all.

Try it for yourself!

Be the Steven Spielberg of your own mind

Find somewhere comfortable to sit, where you won't be disturbed. Breathe slowly and deeply.

Imagine that you are the director of a movie. You have the power to direct the movie exactly as you want. See yourself on the screen and watch yourself going through the scenario you are nervous or anxious about. See yourself in the movie, saying exactly what you need to say and acting confidently, calmly and exactly as you wish. You could rehearse what you want to say out loud. Watch the scene right through until the event is over and you have acted exactly as you wanted.

Now rewind the scene and ask yourself what you could do to make it even better. Then run it through again. This time sit nearer to the action and make the colours brighter. Make the picture bigger and more vivid. Make the dialogue clearer and notice how you are doing everything exactly as you would wish.

Now rewind the scene again in your mind. This time, step into the scene. You are no longer watching and have become part of the movie in your mind. Feel yourself acting exactly as you want. Go right through until you are outside after the event, having done your best.

Repeat until you feel in control of the scene, and that you've given your very best performance.

Notice how you feel now that you know what you want to say and how you want to feel and act.

When you are faced now with the scenario that you fear, your brain will remember your mind movie, and will know what you need to do.

If you have something specific that you want to say, then using this technique is brilliant for rehearsing. Stand in front of a mirror, or practice role-playing with a friend/your coach until you are totally comfortable with the words you want to say, and the message you want to communicate.

Imagine that you are preparing for a business meeting

Another way to reduce your emotional reactions is to view every meeting or piece of correspondence as a business meeting. Set an intention to only say or write things that you would be happy to say or write to a colleague or someone you were negotiating with in a work environment. This will help you to distance yourself from any emotional response you might have.

Using these techniques together will give you a toolkit to maintain your confidence and poise in any situation you might face, however tricky. Make sure you practice them, and keep going back to them, as your emotional brain may well try to hijack!

Remember, you are in charge of your mind and you can use all these techniques to remain cool and calm.

The next two chapters will concentrate on how you can support your children through your divorce. If you don't have children, please do skip ahead. If you have adult children, my experience is that sometimes it is easy to assume they are not affected by your break-up – but this isn't always true. Adult children too need support through their parents' break-up, and I hope the tips in the next two chapters will help.

CHAPTER 15

Supporting your Children through Divorce

"Be a wonderful role model, because you will be the window through which many children will see their future" -Thomas McKinnon Weed

So far this book has concentrated on you – and rightly so! You are the one person who will always be there for you, throughout your life.

However, I see a lot of clients who are worried about the impact their divorce may have on their children, and they ask how they can best support their children through the process. Many of the techniques you have used throughout this book work brilliantly with children, with very positive results.

Children learn by modelling the behaviour of the people around them, so when you model behaviours and ways of approaching challenges that focus on the future, your children will follow your lead. By doing the exercises in this book, and focusing on taking responsibility for your life, you are already setting a fabulous example for your children.

When your children see a parent who is calm, and able to control their emotions to respond with dignity in a crisis they learn how to handle stress and challenge, and how to rebuild after trauma. By passing on techniques and ways of thinking and behaving to your children, you empower them to process their emotions and move forward themselves. These are powerful and valuable life lessons!

The choice you have already made to pick up and read this book has, I hope, made a difference to your way of thinking and how you handle life's curveballs. The wonderful reality is that as you model those behaviours and that different way of thinking, it will ripple out to benefit your family.

Listen carefully to your children

Just as you are going through your healing cycle, so too will your children. They too may feel angry, shocked or depressed. Their journey is likely to be different to yours, take different twists and turns, and go at a different speed. As you become more able to face your own fears and emotions, you become more able to hear those around you talk about their feelings and emotions.

My biggest tip is to listen to your children, perhaps share the emotions wheel from Chapter 8 with them, to help them to identify and name their feelings.

Reassure them that their feelings are normal and let them know that how they feel matters to you. Just the process of naming and validating their emotions can go a long way to helping them handle any overwhelm they may be feeling.

Encourage your children to express their feelings, whether that is through talking, role playing, drawing, creating or something else. Whatever works for them, let it be.

Teach them how to breathe to bring calm

The simple breathing techniques I have shared with you throughout this book will also help your children. Teaching them how to breath for relaxation, as I describe in Chapter 6, will help them to feel calm. The Your Breath is more Powerful than your Thoughts technique from Chapter 7 will give them a powerful tool to use whenever they feel overwhelmed or anxious, or scared by any of the strong feelings that they may feel.

Help your children to find the upside

I worked with a mum recently whose daughter was finding it very difficult to adjust to life after her parents' relationship broke down. My client felt that she wasn't best equipped to help her daughter handle her emotions at a time when she too felt bereft and low.

We worked together to find the upside, and to reframe how my client could look at her situation so that she could see a different, more positive perspective.

You can help your children to do this too. Try asking your child:

- If there was just one upside to this, what would it be?
- If you could see a silver lining, what would it be?
- What are you glad about today?
- What can you do now that wasn't possible before?
- What happened today that cheered you up?

These are fabulous questions that will help your child to shift their focus onto what they CAN do, rather than what they can't. Add their answers to your gratitude board, or list of good things, or write them on post-it notes around the house, so that you are constantly reminded of the upside.

My client's daughter responded that she enjoyed going swimming with Daddy on her own last week, and that they'd had fun in the park on Saturday. She was also enjoying the opportunity to do more craft activities with her Mum when they had time together.

Your child might resist and say there is nothing good about this at all. If this happens, be confident and persevere - "I know it might not be obvious, but if there *was* one good thing about this, what would it be?" Give them examples of the upsides you can find and watch them follow your lead.

Make the time you DO have count

It can be easy to focus on the time you are losing with your children. I always encourage my clients to turn this around. Just as you need to plan to do things you enjoy in the time your children are away at their other parent's, make plans for the time when you do have your children with you.

Keep a list of things you can do together that you love, and that help you all to feel better. When my children were little, we used to love going to the beach to collect stones and to jump in the waves on the shore or go for a walk in the woods to climb on tree trunks and jump in puddles. What do you love to do?

If you look for opportunities to explore and try new things, they will too. If you focus on what you can do rather than what you can't, so will they. They will follow your lead.

Often, holidays are a worry for my clients. Consider creating a holiday bucket list of things you'd like to do or try over the holidays. Choose two or three to commit to and plan them into your schedule. When you do them, take lots of photos and create a new memory board for your house of all the things you have enjoyed doing together.

Show them how to change how they feel in the blink of an eye

In Chapter 9, I showed you how you can change how you feel very quickly by changing how you stand, or by doing something to break the power of a negative state. This is a really simple technique to share with your children. Sometimes, all that is needed is a set of 5 star jumps and a whoop to kickstart a change in mood. Most kids love to smile and laugh, so try doing something silly or fun. When you smile and laugh together, you send endorphins around your body, and it makes a huge difference to how you feel.

Show them how to be in 'control of the clicker'

"Whenever I'd complain or was upset about something in my own life, my mother had the same advice – darling, just change the channel. You are in control of the clicker. Don't replay the bad, scary movie" -Arianna Huffington

Remember, your brain will try to answer the questions you ask it, and the same is true of your children's brains. Go back to your list of better questions, and use them with your children:

- What would my best friend advise me right now?
- What would help me to feel better today?
- What am I grateful for today?
- What choices do I have right now?
- What have I done that I am proud of?

Just as you have written your questions onto post-it notes and stuck them up around your house, so too can your children. Asking these questions will encourage them to model the resilience that you are showing yourself.

I recently asked my eldest son what he felt he had learnt from the years he has spent living between my house and his dad's. He replied that he feels he is adaptable, organised and independent. Those are all resources he will now have for life. Far from being a "damaged" child from a "broken home", he is a rounded, adaptable, independent and optimistic teen. And I am incredibly proud.

Your children will take their cue from you. If you are down and negative, they will be too. If you are angry and resentful, they are likely to feel conflicted and stressed. By contrast, when you are upbeat and make plans to do things together, they will do the same. You can do this regardless of how your ex behaves. You can be the role model you want to be for your children in the time they spend with you. I promise you that it will pay dividends in the years to come.

CHAPTER 16

Parenting together through Divorce and Beyond

In the last chapter I suggested ways in which you can support your children through this period of change in their lives, to help them develop techniques and strategies that they can use whenever something happens.

One of my main concerns when my marriage broke down was how my ex-husband and I would parent our children successfully. Parenting apart had not been part of my life-plan, and at first, I felt overwhelmed, lost and confused. I googled, devoured information on the internet, and took in advice from all kinds of experts. From the very beginning, the one thing I did know was that I did not want our divorce to have a damaging effect on our children.

Over the decade since our split, we have worked out a way to be parents to our children that (mostly!) works for us. Our boys divide their time approximately 60/40 between our respective homes. Both my ex-husband and I are remarried, so they have step-parents at both houses. They also have a younger brother with their dad and step-mum, and older step-siblings in my second husband's grown-up children. Our children are in their teens now, and our approach is shifting again as they develop social lives of their own (which are far more exciting than ours!).

The journey has not been without challenge, but our children are happy and settled, and have learnt a great deal from watching the way we have worked together for their benefit. They are very far from being the "damaged" children from a "broken home" that the media often portrays.

Be the best role model you can be

I always tell my clients that the important thing to remember is to put the children's interests first. What is going to help them the most? What will your children learn from the way you communicate with your ex? As always, look for the upside, the positives in the situation. Your children will learn from the behaviours that you model to them.

For example, when you can co-parent successfully, they will learn all kinds of life lessons in communication, compromise, flexibility and give-and-take. If you have a challenging ex and need to set very firm guidelines around contact with you, then they will see you setting boundaries and maintaining dignity. If they see a relationship full of conflict, what will they learn?

Of course, you cannot control what your ex does and says, only your responses and reactions (which of course may result in changes in their behaviour). I always say to my clients that whatever your ex does, however badly he or she behaves, you can be the best role model you can be for your children in the time that they are with you.

What you do and say now will set the tone for the years to come. How do you want to feel when you look back in 5 years' time and you recall what you did and said?

In Chapter 14, you created a vision for your future relationship with your ex. Now it is time to create a powerful vision of how you want your parenting relationship with your ex to look and feel. This will give you a compelling goal to work towards, that you can always keep in the forefront of your mind. Bear in mind that your vision for your parenting relationship may be very different to your vision for your personal relationship with your ex.

Use this exercise to start thinking about your vision for your parenting relationship with your ex.

> **Create a vision for your parenting relationship**
>
> Take a big piece of paper, and jot down your thoughts about these questions:
>
> - What do you want your parenting relationship to look and feel like in 6 months/1 year?
> - What do you want your parenting relationship to look and feel like in 5 years?

- What do you want it to look and feel like at your child's wedding/graduation?
- How do you want your children to feel about how you behave?

Once you have a clear vision, keep it at the forefront of your mind, and ask yourself whether what you are about to do or say will bring you closer or further away from that vision.

If possible, share your vision with your ex. When you are working together towards a common, defined goal, it helps to focus the mind on where you are headed. Keep that shared goal at the forefront of your mind in all your discussions and refer back to it.

This long-term vision of your future parenting relationship can keep you on track when things get a bit heated, or your ex does something that you don't agree with. It refocuses you on what you have both agreed is important. If you have been able to agree a shared parenting vision, you can remind both yourself and your ex about your agreed joint goal.

My ex and I agree that the emotional wellbeing of our children is paramount, and that we want our children to know that at their major life events, we will both be there for them. This shared goal informs our communication, whether that is by email, text, phone or face to face.

Of course, it may not be possible to sit down and have this conversation with your ex. If that is the case for you, then having your own personal vision can be just as powerful. When you know what you are trying to achieve, and you keep that vision in the front of your mind, it can stop you from doing things you may later regret.

If you are caught in a cycle of conflict, then sometimes it just takes one of you to step away, and break the cycle, for things to shift and change.

Be consistent

I recently asked my ex-husband what his top tip for successful co-parenting would be. His reply:

"*Always back each other up in front of the children, even when you might not understand the reason behind a decision from the other house. Children need and value consistency from both parents.*"

Where you can, try to agree on a consistent approach across both houses and a joint message that you will both give. On fundamental issues of parenting like mobile phones, use of the internet, general acceptable behaviour, my ex-husband and I try our best to agree on a strategy.

Sometimes you may find that you can't agree on a strategy, or you have totally different opinions and you can't find a middle ground.

If we can't agree on a strategy, then I always say to our children that sometimes parents have different viewpoints. This would happen if their dad and I were still married. Sometimes, what might be OK here isn't OK at dad's and vice versa. They can cope with different rules, so long as their dad and I are consistent in our support of each other.

Keep the children out of any conflict between you

Research shows that divorce is most damaging for children when they are caught up in conflict between their parents. Your children love you both, they don't want to be caught in the middle, or to have to choose between you. There's nothing more uncomfortable for a child than to hear their parents criticising each other in a way that he/she just doesn't understand.

If you do have disagreements or arguments, avoid discussing those with the children, and don't lean on them for emotional support. Don't ask them to take sides or use them to pass messages between you.

Remember to go back and use the techniques in Chapter 14 on communication to help you handle potential conflict.

What would help you to maintain calm when things look like they may get heated? I like to imagine myself with really sloping shoulders and wearing a shiny, slippery coat whenever I need to have any particularly tricky conversation about the children – any aggressive words or inflammatory remarks simply slide off my shoulders and are repelled by my shiny, slippery coat.

I also remind myself that my ex loves our children and wants the best for them as much as I do. When I keep that in the forefront of my mind, it helps me to stay calm and focused on what matters.

One of my clients has an imaginary space helmet that she puts on, which repels aggression and negativity, so that she feels safe. Another imagines herself surrounded by a protective bubble, and another has an inner Readybrek glow that she uses to feel confident and strong.

I also keep the mantra "kids first, ego last" in my mind, and remind myself that it isn't about me. It's about them, and what is best for them.

Remember it's about them, not you

In the beginning it was painful when I had to wave my boys off for a weekend with their dad. In the early days, when I was angry with him, it would have been easy to punish him for hurting me by being difficult about his time with our children.

I always tell myself that our children are 50% of both of us. They need and deserve a good relationship with both of us. Whatever I was feeling in the early days, I plastered a smile on my face as they drove off for time at their dad's. They didn't need to see my pain or worry about me when they were away. They needed to be free to have a strong bond with us both.

Take a helicopter view

I outlined this exercise earlier, in Chapter 14 on communication, so if you used it then, it will be familiar to you.

Sometimes when emotions are running high, it can be hard to see the wood for the trees. If you are caught in a fight over holiday times or there is an issue that is causing a problem, take a helicopter view and see what comes up for you. I have adjusted the exercise to include looking at the situation from your children's perspective.

Take a Helicopter View

First bring the issue to mind and summarise it in just a couple of sentences.

- What is your perspective? How do you feel? What do you want to achieve? What is important to you?

Stand up and shake your body. Move into a different chair, or a different spot in the room.

- Imagine you are your ex. Really imagine being them, with their values, experiences and views. What is your perspective? How do you feel? What do you want to achieve? What is important to you?

Stand up again and shake your body. Move again into a different chair or spot in the room.

- Imagine now that you are your child/children. Really feel into being them. What do they want? How do they feel? What key message do they have for you?

Stand up again and shake your body.

- Now imagine you are an independent third party, watching from a helicopter hovering overhead. You can clearly see and hear everything that you, your ex and your children have just said about how they feel. What do you notice?

Once you have stepped out of the helicopter, take a moment to take in all this information. How has your perspective shifted? What new insights have you gained?

How could you use your new insights and perspective as you discuss your plans with your ex?

Focus on what you CAN do, not what you can't

Many of you will find it challenging to send your children off to your ex's house. I know I did at first. Perhaps this will be the first time you have spent longer than a few nights away from your children, or maybe you feel resentful about the time you are not spending with them. Or perhaps you dread each weekend they are away, as you don't enjoy the time alone and you feel lost.

One way to turn down the temperature on those emotions is to focus on what you CAN do and CAN have, rather than on what you can't. Take back your power over your time and your feelings.

Ask yourself questions like:

- What can I do in that time that I couldn't do before?
- What have I always wanted to do and never had the time?
- Who do I know who handles this well? What can I learn from them?
- Who can I arrange to meet up with to have some child free time?
- What do I love to do and enjoy? When could I do more of that?

Be open to opportunities. When you shift your focus onto what you can do instead of what you can't, you can change how you feel about the time you have away from the children, and this will impact your discussions with your ex.

I hope that you are seeing great results from the techniques you have used so far, to help you focus on moving forward positively. It may be worth taking a moment now to reflect on just how far you've come, and how much you have overcome. Because it's time now to start the really exciting part – redefining who you are!

CHAPTER 17

Know What You Value

"You are not what happens to you. You are who you choose to become!" -Karl Jung

This is where it gets exciting! Although divorce or separation is an ending, it is also a beginning. It is the beginning of the rest of your life. Wherever there is change, however painful, there is opportunity.

You can use your divorce as a catalyst to do something amazing. You can grow, learn, try new ways of doing things or redefine yourself. You can create the sparkling life you want.

As my clients go through their divorce journeys, they often say to me that they aren't sure who they are any more. It is so easy to lose touch with aspects of yourself in a marriage or relationship, as you compromise and shift to fit being part of a couple.

All of the strategies and techniques in this book are designed to help you to reach a place where you are ready to move on and rediscover yourself. By focusing on you, by becoming clear and making choices to take positive steps forward, you are building yourself up and taking control of your divorce process. These are skills you now have for life, and you can use them to start visualising and creating your new life and your new brilliant future.

It really can be life-changing. Some of my clients have gone on to get big promotions at work, set up new businesses, go on great adventures such as walking el Camino de Santiago and redefine their relationship with themselves. You too have an amazing opportunity now to get to know yourself again and explore your values and dreams and then create a life around them.

This might be the first time that you've really explored who you are, and what you value.

It certainly was for me. I had daydreamed my way into marriage without really checking in with myself as to whether it was what I really wanted, or who I really was. We had been together since we were 21 and in our final year at university. All our friends were getting married, we had been together for 7 years and it was the next step on the socially accepted ladder.

Perhaps it feels a bit daunting or overwhelming to try to envisage a new future, so we'll break it into chunks and decide on steps that you can achieve. The first step is to explore what you value and what really matters to you.

What are your values?

When I talk about values, I mean those things that fundamentally really matter to you. They are those things that you want to create your life around. They are the principles that are most important to you and they affect how you think, feel and behave. They are what makes you tick, what motivates you and they influence your decisions and choices. When you know what you really value, you can knowingly create a life that honours those values, and you can use them to help you make decisions and choices.

They will change with your life, as you change, or things happen to you. Knowing your values is an ongoing thing – so I suggest you reassess them regularly.

For example, my current top value is freedom. To me, freedom is being able to do the things I love with the people I love. It is the freedom to travel, experience new things, and explore new places and activities, learn new things and expand my world. Without that, I feel small, trapped, closed in and overwhelmed. To a large degree, it's perhaps why I have set up my own business – so that I am free to run it the way I feel best, and in the way that feels right in conjunction with my second highest value, integrity.

I have developed a values discovery exploration exercise that I love to go through with clients. It has its basis in NLP and I have also taken inspiration from the work of other fellow coaches including Ebonie Allard and Lindsay West.

The exercise below is designed to help you discover your own personal values, and what is important for you to create your life around.

Discovering your values

Read the instructions through first before getting going. Alternatively, you might find it helpful to go through this exercise with someone to jot down the words you say.

- Get a big piece of paper and write "What is important to me in life?" in the middle/at the top. This is a huge question, so brainstorm any answers that come to mind. You might write "my children", "my work", "fun", "holidays" etc. At this point, write down anything and everything that comes to mind. Many of these will be things, rather than values, but they are all important as they give you clues as to what really matters to you.

- For each of the things you've written down on your page, ask yourself what does that give me or enable me to be? This question helps you to identify the value behind the thing that is important to you. Jot down any words that come to mind. Keep asking yourself "What else does that give me or enable me to be, that's even better?" until you can think of nothing greater.

This will take you to the underlying values beneath – for example, your dog gives you connection or unconditional love. Your career perhaps gives you money (which is not a value in itself), and money in turn might give you security.

- Think of a time now when you felt totally happy. Close your eyes and see yourself in that scene, feeling really happy. Where were you? Who was there with you? What were you doing? What did you see, hear and feel? Jot down any words that come to mind.

- Now ask yourself, what did that give you, or enable you to be? Again this question helps you to identify the value behind the happiness – what at your core meant this memory is so powerful? Keep asking the same question – what else did that give you or enable you to be that was even better? – until you can think of nothing better.

- Next think of a time when you felt truly fulfilled. Close your eyes and see yourself in that scene, feeling totally fulfilled. Where were you? Who was there with you? What were you doing? What did you see, hear and feel? Jot down any words that come to mind.

- Again, ask yourself what that gave you or enabled you to be? Keep asking, what else did that give you or enable you to be that's even better?

- Now think of a time when you felt really proud. Close your eyes and see yourself in that scene, feeling proud. Where were you? Who was there with you? What were you doing? What did you see, hear and feel? Jot down any words that come to mind.

- Again, ask yourself what that gave you or enabled you to be? Keep asking, what else did that give you or enable you to be that's even better?

- You will now have a page or two full of words that describe what is important to you.

Before we go on to prioritising your values, I want to give you a couple of examples.

One of my clients said that her happy memory was of being on the beach with her family and dog on a hot day. The children were playing, the water was calm, there was no wind and she could hear laughter. The memory gave her a feeling of easy calm which was peaceful and relaxed. That gave her a feeling of being energised and enabled her to feel connected to her family. That connection gave her a feeling of security and safety, so that she could be truly herself. Her deep value lay in feeling that she could be 'Truly Me'.

Another client said that he felt most fulfilled when he had designed and built a wooden sideboard in his workshop. He felt creative and that he was pushing himself to design something truly beautiful. That gave him a feeling of satisfaction and pride, that he was creating and challenging himself. That gave him a feeling of deep peacefulness. He felt at one with nature and the world. His value lay in being connected.

Another told me about how proud she was that she had lost 5 stone, through hard work and effort. She was proud of her determination to succeed, and of her will power. She enjoyed the feeling of accomplishment and achievement, and of overcoming the odds. She ultimately concluded that she valued rising to a challenge.

Prioritising your values

Not all of the things you value will be as important as each other, so the next step is to identify which values are most important to you. The first step towards this is to narrow your value words down to 10.

- Go through all the words on your sheets of paper. Which ones are fundamental? Which do you feel you could not live without? Circle the values which you feel are most important to you.

- Identify any that easily group together. For example, you may feel that honesty, integrity and trust go together in one group and adventure, fun and exploration go in another.

- Keep narrowing the words down until you have 10 words or groups of words that go together.

- Now that you have your top 10 values let's put them in order. You could write each one on a post-it note and move the post-it notes around until you feel they are in the right order for you. A good question to ask yourself when you're comparing values to see which are more important is, "if I had to choose one out of A or B, which could I live <u>without</u> for the rest of my life?". The answer to this will give you a sense of how to prioritise your values.

How can you use your list of values?

You can use your list of values in all kinds of ways to help you remember them and stay focused on them.

Firstly, put them where you can see them! There are many ways you could do this – perhaps write them on post-it notes and stick them up. Or write them on a piece of paper and keep it in your purse or wallet or next to your bed. Share them with your friends and family and talk about them in general conversation.

Or you could create a vision board that reflects your values visually – give it a go and put your board up somewhere you will see it all the time.

Create a vision board

Take a big piece of card, and a load of magazines or photos. Cut out pictures and words that remind you of your values and stick them on the card. Use images and words that inspire and motivate you and represent your values.

Put your board up where you can see it regularly and remind yourself of what really matters to you. You could also include quotes or belief statements too. Doing this helps you to keep your values fresh and in the forefront of your mind.

You could do this online too, using pinterest for example.

Use your values to help you make decisions

Once you know what your values are, start to include them in your decision-making. For example, if honesty is your top value, ask yourself "Am I being honest with myself here?" and "What would be the honest thing to do?". If freedom is high on your list, ask yourself "Will making this choice take away or increase my freedom?".

As Tony Robbins has said, "When you know what's most important to you, making a decision is quite simple. Most people, though, are unclear about what is most important in their lives, and thus decision making becomes a form of internal torture". When you use your values to inform your decision-making, it becomes much easier, and you can be true to you.

Once you know what your values are, use these questions to check in with yourself, and whether you are living in accordance with them.

Are you living in accordance with your values?

For each of your top three values, ask yourself:

- On a scale of 1-10 how far am I living in accordance with that value right now?
- Would I like to increase or decrease the presence of this value in my life?
- What small steps could I take to achieve that?

Now that you know what matters to you, and what you value, it's time to start to plan your new life! The next chapter will help you begin to do this, if you haven't already found yourself doing so!

Let's start creating your new, vibrant life – to reflect you, and your values.

CHAPTER 18

Creating your Vibrant New Life

"Because I'm worth it"
–Ilon Specht, L'Oreal Paris, 1973

Now that you know what really matters to you and the values you want to create your new life around, let's look at ways you can start to create that life. This is the exciting part – it's where the magic happens!

I often find that clients are very clear on what they want to move away from – perhaps the pain of betrayal, resentment, anger and hurt – but not so clear on where they want to get to. This chapter is all about creating some compelling goals that you are moving towards which will help you create the life you want.

Perhaps it feels as though creating a new life is a really daunting, scary, unknown thing. Let's break it down into manageable steps. Remember, as Martin Luther King said, "You don't have to see the whole staircase – just take the first step".

Show yourself that you are worth it

Go back to your list of things that you enjoy doing that you made in Chapter 7. Have you been doing those things? What difference do you notice after you do them? How did you feel?

If you haven't been doing them, ask yourself why not? Were they the right things? Did they really float your boat? Or did they feel too much back then? How could you introduce or increase them now?

At first, my intention in asking you to do the things on your list was to help you shift your focus back onto you and to show yourself that you are worth it. As you do more of the things you enjoy, notice how it changes your approach to your days.

What can you do now that wasn't possible before?

Already during your progress through this book, you will have considered this question, and thought of things that you can do now that you couldn't do before. Whether they are small things or huge things, they are all contributing to the creation of your new and exciting life.

It's time now to really take this question to another level and start to dream about the life you want to live – a life that is built around your values, and which nourishes and excites you. As you begin to dream about creating your new life, you may be surprised at what comes up, and how you start to feel differently.

I was recently working with a client, Luke, who was caught up in resentment. He had been divorced for several years and felt angry that he had given away too much in his divorce settlement. Luke felt frustrated, angry and resentful – and those feelings were keeping him stuck in a state of anxiety and regret. He was stuck in past hurt and resentment.

When we started to talk about his values and the vision he had for his future life, he found that as he made plans for his future, the more excited he became, and the less he felt the old resentment and anger. He called his new plans his magnet, pulling him forward. In the end, Luke realised that had it not been for his divorce, he would not be making any of these plans, and he was now free to follow some of his dreams. What a brilliant reframe! Although the financial settlement he had agreed to had not been ideal for him, he knew he could not change it, and so he chose not to dwell on that any longer. Instead he chose to put his energy into creating a new life that he found fulfilling.

Take a bird's eye view of your life

Many coaches use the "Wheel of Life" tool to help clients take a big picture view of their life. The Wheel of Life is a circle, divided into segments, each representing an area of your life that is important to you. I like to divide mine into eight, but you could use 6 or 10.

The aim of the Wheel of Life is to give you a clear visual of where your life is in balance, where you are satisfied, and where you would like to make changes. Give it a go for yourself.

Wheel of Life

On a piece of paper, draw a circle and divide into 8 segments. Each segment will represent an area of your life. For example, you could choose to include:

- Work
- Relationship
- Family
- Friends/social life
- Community
- Health
- Money/finances
- Fun/leisure
- Personal growth/development
- Home
- Your top values as separate segments

Include anything that is important to you.

For each segment, draw a line to mark across the segment to reflect how satisfied you are with that area out of 10, with 0 being the middle of the circle, and 10 being at the outside.

Once you have drawn lines for each segment, you will see that your wheel is joined up.

What do you notice about your wheel? Is it balanced, or are there bumps in your wheel? Would it give a smooth ride if it were a wheel on a bicycle? Where would you like to concentrate on making changes or focusing your efforts?

Take the segments with the lowest scores and ask yourself where you would like that line to be. If you have given a segment a 4/10 for example, would you like that to become a 6 or 8? Or a 10?

Now jot down 2 or 3 actions you could take to improve that area. How could you get more clarity? Who might you be able to ask for help? What could you do to start making changes? Remember if you keep doing the same thing, you will keep getting the same results, so ask yourself what you could do differently to achieve a better outcome.

Also look at the segments with the higher scores and ask yourself whether you would like those areas to be even better. What could you do to achieve that? What are you doing that is already working, that you could do more of?

Dreaming and goal setting

I like to encourage my clients to dream big. When you start to imagine, visualise, think about and take steps towards goals that motivate, excite and inspire you, you can end up doing things that you once believed impossible. I have had clients who have done amazing things as a result of allowing themselves to dream. One is walking the Camino de Santiago by herself, another has set up a new business, and another has taken a big promotion at work – one that she previously thought was way beyond her capabilities.

I was working with a client on this recently and she started off by saying that she wanted to have a party to celebrate that she was moving into her new house.

Her ex-husband didn't enjoy entertaining and she had been looking forward to organising a party for a long time. As we moved through the session, her dreams got bigger and she mentioned that in her 20s she had lived in Milan and dreamt of having freedom to travel and see the world. This was now a dream that she could re-kindle and she began to talk about climbing Kilimanjaro and visiting India.

Take some time to daydream and imagine your new life using this exercise.

Dare to dream

Take a blank page in your notebook and brainstorm whatever comes to mind in answer to these questions:

- What have you always wanted to do, but couldn't do before?
- What would you do if you knew you couldn't fail?
- What did your 20-year-old self-dream of doing?
- What will your 70-year-old self-regret not doing?
- If you could wave a magic wand and wake up tomorrow in your ideal world, what would it look like? What would you see, hear and feel?
- If you found a genie in a bottle, what 3 things would you wish to be, do or have in your life?

At this moment, don't censor your thoughts. Just write down whatever comes to mind. It doesn't matter if they seem unrealistic just now, write them down anyway. They can be big or small. You might include places you want to visit, people you want to reconnect with, hobbies you'd like to try, new foods you'd like to taste or jobs you might like to do.

Now look through your brainstorm and choose 2 or 3 that you would like to investigate further.

For each of the goals you have chosen, ask yourself:

- What will that give me or allow me to be?
- What will that give me or allow me to be that's even better?

Keep asking the second question over and over, until you can't think of anything better. This will help you to understand *why* this goal is so important. If you know *why* it is important, you are much more likely to be motivated to achieve it.

You may find that you keep ending up in the same place or with similar words. Whenever I do this, I always end up at freedom and exploration. I know that those things motivate me so my goals often involve travel or trying new experiences.

For each of your chosen goals, write down 3-5 small steps that you can take, right now, to start to move towards achieving them. It doesn't matter how small the steps are, just so long as they will take you that little bit closer to your goal.

If one of your goals is to sort out your garden, your steps could be a) get into the habit of mowing the lawn once a week, b) research what flowers would grow well in the type of soil in your garden and c) invite some friends round to help you clear the flowerbeds, and afterwards have a few drinks and a barbecue.

If your dream is to travel solo around South America, you might decide to a) research which 2 or 3 countries you most want to visit, b) buy a Lonely Planet guide and c) talk to your friend who spent a month in Argentina.

By taking this step by step approach you are making your goals achievable. Taking small steps means that you won't become overwhelmed and you will feel that you are moving forward. By taking lots of small steps forwards, you'll soon be able to look back and see how much you can achieve.

Be adventurous and try new things

Divorce gives you the opportunity to try all sorts of new things. If, like me, you have children, they are likely to spend chunks of time with their other parent. Suddenly you have time to try new things, meet new people and reinvent who you are. I joined a cycling club and learned to dance – both activities I would have loved to have had time for whilst I was married!

Trying these new things, finding that I enjoyed them and was good at them, gave me a boost and fostered my confidence and independence – both of which also helped me to navigate my divorce. I also found new friends and built a new independent social life. Now I treasure my 'childfree' weekends as I can indulge in the activities that I love.

Know that you have the power!

Through using the tools in this book, and others you may have picked up along the way, you know now that you hold the power to create your life. You, and only you can effect these changes, by consciously taking control, and investing in you and in your future. Remember how you now use your WOW brain rather than your OW brain? If you've forgotten, go back to the "Use your WOW brain" technique in Chapter 10. It will help you now as you look back and notice just how far you've come.

You could cement this by looking back over the last few months and making a list or brainstorm of all the things you have achieved and overcome. Note down all the things you have done to make things better for yourself, all the times that you made a choice and decided to do something differently.

Notice that YOU did that.

As you continue your journey, notice that each time you make a new decision, or choose a different way, it gets easier, and you become more confident. It is worth it! You are worth it! You have the rest of your life ahead of you and I know you aren't going to let it be defined by your divorce.

CHAPTER 19

Letting Go

*"Holding on to anger is like drinking poison, and
expecting someone else to die" –anonymous*

Shifting your focus onto creating your new life moving
forward will help to propel you forward.
Understanding your values and nurturing ideas and
goals for your new life will mean you focus on the
future, and on moving forward positively. That is all
wonderful and exciting – but what if, like many of my
clients, there are still feelings of anger, resentment or
bitterness that still lurk, stopping you from moving
forward fully into your new life?

The very sudden and unexpected end to my
marriage threw my whole world into question. It
made me doubt the very fabric of the life I had built
and that I had believed we had built together. I
questioned myself, my worth and my value. I asked
why he didn't love me enough to stay faithful, or even

to talk to me about how he felt. Perhaps this is something you recognise in yourself?

Are you finding it a challenge to move beyond resentment? Like the client I mentioned in the last chapter, do you feel bitter at how your life has changed, whilst your ex's life seems to be much more settled? Or perhaps you are struggling to let go of your anger towards your ex for leaving, or for making your negotiations such a challenge.

Whatever it is that you are holding onto, those feelings give the person you are angry with, or resentful towards, a power over your emotions and your life that means you are not fully in the driving seat. Those difficult feelings like anger, resentment and bitterness keep the emotional ties between you alive and they can leave you feeling powerless.

The first step is to imagine a different way. Try this exercise and see what comes up for you.

Imagine life without those feelings

Take a fresh page in your diary, and jot down answers to these questions:

- What would if feel like if I chose to let go of those feelings?
- How would my life be improved?
- What would I be able to feel and think that would be better?
- What would I have space for if those feelings were no longer there?

In my experience, letting go of those feelings means that you can move into your new life with hope, excitement and optimism.

This chapter is all about letting go of any of those residual feelings, so that you can move forward free of them into that wonderful future you are busy creating for yourself.

Understand that letting go is something you do for YOU

As you know, my husband had an affair and left me very suddenly. It would have been so easy to put all the blame for the breakdown of our marriage onto him – his weaknesses, his lack of communication of his unhappiness and his betrayal. Doing that was comforting at first as it meant that people were sympathetic. They told me that he would "come to his senses", that he would realise what a mistake he'd made, that his behaviour was awful and that I didn't deserve what had happened to me. For the first few months, I held onto those feelings as though they were an anchor. They were a kind of anchor in a way - they kept me safe from focusing on myself. They meant I could put all the blame on my ex-husband.

Holding onto all that blame, anger and resentment was only hurting me. It wasn't hurting him. After all, he didn't even know I was feeling it most of the time, except when it exploded out into our communication. And that never ended well, and only resulted in increased stress, anger and blame.

Then one day, I read somewhere that holding onto anger is like drinking poison and expecting someone else to die.

That really resonated with me and has stuck with me ever since. I love the analogy and I believe it's right. The anger or resentment or bitterness that you hold onto eats away at you, it takes time and energy away from the positive steps you could be taking to create your new life.

I realised that letting go of that blame and those feelings was not something that I would be doing for him. I would be doing it for me. By shifting my focus away from my anger and pain, my bitterness and resentment, I would free up my brain space for better things. Therefore, I made a conscious decision to let those feelings go.

Some of you might be thinking "Yeah right, Claire. I hear what you're saying, but HOW do I do that?"

The first step is to be 100% honest with yourself. When you have a good half hour or so to spare, work through this exercise.

Be honest with yourself

What old angry/resentful/bitter feelings or thoughts are you holding onto? Brainstorm them all onto a piece of paper or write them all down in your diary.

- As you write, notice how those thoughts and feelings affect your life. How do they affect:
  - the way you behave?
  - the way you communicate?
  - the way you feel about yourself and your situation?

- Then ask yourself what it is that you gain from those thoughts and feelings?

  This can be a really challenging question. Perhaps those feelings mean that you get sympathy from other people which makes you feel better, or perhaps it means that you don't need to look at your part in what happened, and it is easier to put 100% of the blame onto your ex.

- Now imagine what it would feel like to be able to let go of those old feelings.

  ➢ What would that feel like?
  ➢ What would you be able to do that feels impossible now?
  ➢ What other emotions would you have space for?
  ➢ What difference could it make to your life?

As you jot down answers to these questions, notice what you notice. Feel whatever you feel and be kind to yourself. You may want to come back to the questions again and again. You may want to sleep on it, or talk it through with a trusted friend, or your coach/therapist. Take your time – this is important stuff.

Are you ready now to let go? Try some of the following ideas and see which works for you.

Visualise yourself letting go

You have already started doing this with the exercise above. Look back at your notes and breathe deeply. Close your eyes and imagine being in a life without anger, bitterness or resentment, or whatever the negative emotion is for you. See yourself going about your daily life without the pull of those feelings. Imagine what being free of those feelings will enable you to be, do and feel. Without those feelings, what do you have space for?

Every day, imagine yourself letting go, little by little. Visualise the old feelings seeping out of your body and washing away, soaking into the ground and disappearing.

You could create a vision board for your life now that it is free of those feelings, full of pictures and words that represent that freedom to you. Go back to Chapter 17 to remind yourself how to start putting a vision board together.

Breathe out your anger into a balloon

Buy a pack of balloons. If you can, get rocket balloons. They are long and thin, and once you blow them up, you can let them go and they whizz off into the air where they swirl and squeal and dance.

Blow up the balloons and imagine that you are blowing all of your anger/resentment into the balloon. When you let the balloon go, watch them dance and whizz, and imagine all that anger dissipating in the wind.

Use the Feelings Buster technique

Remember how you changed your feelings in Chapter 9 using the Feelings Buster technique? That technique will really help you now. You can take your feelings and change them by changing how you see them or feel them or hear them, by making them softer or smaller, quieter or dimmer, or even by choosing to throw them away.

Write all your hurt onto pebbles and throw them in the sea

I am lucky enough to live near the sea and a pebbly beach and I find this a very powerful technique. Take a pen and sit on the beach. Write your hurts, your resentment, your bitterness onto pebbles. For example – "I am angry that you left me". Take each pebble and throw it as hard as you can into the water. As you throw say "I am letting go of my anger".

You could do this on paper, then shred or burn it.

Whatever way you decide to do this, the important thing is that you are making a conscious decision to let go, symbolically throwing the old emotion away.

Write a "letting go letter"

Write a letter to your ex, telling them that you are letting go of all the blame, resentment and bitterness. Tell them how that is going to improve your life.

When you write this letter, it is important that you mean it and that it is sincere. It might be something that you do a bit later, once you have used some of the other techniques.

The aim of this letter is not to send it. Your ex will never know that you have written it. Instead, keep it for yourself and read it every day. Notice how each time you read it your feelings shift.

The combination of letting go and focusing on your values and new life is a powerful one. When you truly let go, it frees you up to create a new reality free of emotional baggage. This doesn't mean that you will never again feel sadness or regret, or that your ex will never do something again that makes you feel angry. What it does mean is that you will be free to concentrate on living your life without a cloud hanging over you. You will be able to put all your focus into creating your new life, and you'll have space to explore new and exciting options and choices.

Making space for those new feelings and options may present all sorts of opportunities for you. Often, my clients find that about now is when they start to imagine having someone new in their lives. After all, you've let go of your baggage, you know what you want to create your new life around, and you've got plans and goals that you dream of and are taking steps towards. Perhaps you are beginning to feel that you may be ready for a new relationship.

CHAPTER 20

New
Relationships

"Know who you are. Know what you want. Know what you deserve. And never settle for less than you deserve" – Tony Gaskins

Now that you have all the resources you need to focus on creating your new life without the baggage of the past, you may find yourself looking forward to a new relationship. As you emerge from your break-up, you have a wonderful opportunity to focus on exactly what you want from any new relationship, whether that be a new friendship, or a new romantic relationship. You can enter any new relationship as a different you, the you that you have discovered as a part of this process – and that is so exciting!

This chapter is all about knowing what you need and want and maximising your opportunities to succeed in a new relationship!

Know your boundaries

Deepak Chopra defines boundaries in a relationship as "clearly established parameters of emotional, physical and mental space that we expect others to respect in the relationships they have with us". He describes them as being like a screen door, which allows a cool breeze to come in whilst keeping leaves and insects out. The screen door is yours to control – you can decide whether and how far you open it. Notice that if you open it too far, the leaves and insects will come in, and you may struggle to close it again.

Your boundaries define what you will and will not tolerate in any relationship. It is important to know where your boundaries are, and what you will and will not accept – and what you are prepared to do should someone overstep your boundaries. When you have clear boundaries and you feel confident in communicating them, you can protect your values, and stand up for yourself.

Many of us find this really challenging – perhaps you feel guilty when you say no, or you are afraid of the consequences of disagreeing. Or you have learnt over a lifetime that others' needs are more important than your own, or maybe it was just easier to give in.

How do you know where your boundaries are?

Have you ever had a feeling, a sense that there is something wrong, or felt uncomfortable, anxious, resentful, or angry about something a partner or friend has said or done? You may not be able to put your finger on it, but you know something just doesn't "feel right"? Or perhaps you find yourself rushing around meeting everyone else's needs but feel exhausted and overwhelmed yourself.

These sorts of feelings often signal that a boundary has been violated in some way.

Think back to past relationships to get clues about your boundaries.

Identifying your boundaries

Think back to your past relationships:

- Were there times when you let your partner or friend treat you in a way you did not like?
- Did that person do or say things that made you feel uncomfortable or resentful?
- Did you start off making compromises that over time felt more like sacrifices?
- Did your gut sometimes tell you something was amiss, but you ignored it and regretted it later?
- Did you feel responsible for the other person's feelings if you said no?

Jot down your answers to these questions, as they will give you clues as to where your boundaries lie.

Once you have done that, make a list of the boundaries you would like to put in place in your future relationships.

Communicating your boundaries

Once you know where your boundaries are, you can use this information to notice when someone might be overstepping one or more of your boundaries. The next step is to communicate those boundaries, and to feel confident in doing so.

You can practice communicating your boundaries, perhaps standing in front of a mirror or with a trusted friend or your coach/therapist.

Practice communicating your boundaries

First, take a moment to imagine what life would be like if you were able to communicate your boundaries:

- What would be different?
- What would you be able to do?
- How would you feel differently about yourself and your relationships?

State your boundary clearly, calmly, firmly and respectfully. Talk from the "I" when you feel one of your boundaries has been crossed. For example, "When you call me when I am at work, I am unable to answer so please call me after 6 once you know I will be home".

Remember that the other person's response is their responsibility – not yours. If your new boyfriend wants to see you every night, and you don't want to commit to that amount of time, it is not your responsibility to deal with his disappointment, or to appease him. His feelings are his to handle, not yours.

It is however, your responsibility to communicate your boundary to others.

> Using the above example, you could say "When you want to see me every day, I feel pressured and that I am being rushed, so I would like to keep our relationship to three nights a week".
>
> Don't start with "I'm sorry but...", as this undermines what you are about to say, and suggests that you feel bad or guilty about the boundary you are setting.
>
> Practice! If setting boundaries is new to you, start small. It might feel awkward the first time you do it, and some people may not like it – especially if they are used to you behaving in a certain way.

The clearer you are in your communication, the easier your interactions will be and the easier it will be to see choices and make decisions about your relationships. You could revisit Chapter 14 on communication to remind yourself of how you can already communicate effectively.

If someone repeatedly oversteps your boundaries, despite clear communication from you, then remember you have choices. You can choose for example to stop seeing that person, or to set it out again, or you can decide to be flexible with that boundary. Remember, though, that when you are flexible with a boundary, it can be a challenge to reinstate that boundary later, should you wish to!

One of my clients, Alison, recently messaged me to say that she had met a man at a speed dating session, and they had arranged to meet up afterwards. It would have been her first date in over 30 years. Shortly before the date, he messaged to say that he had to postpone. Alison's friends suggested that perhaps he had a meeting or was visiting a sick relative or was attending a charity event. Notice how these were all excuses they were creating to try to make Alison feel better! However, Alison knew that she was worth more than this so she responded to say that although she was disappointed not to meet up, as she had thought he was lovely, someone else would be getting her first date. She wished him well and signed off.

Alison could have made any number of different decisions in this scenario, but she made the decision that was most in line with her top value of being 'Truly Me' and having confidence in her own self-worth. She did not want to date someone who, right from the beginning, did not prioritise their date.

Know what makes you feel loved

Before you consider a new relationship, it is worth thinking about what you want and need in your relationships. How do you want to be loved? How do you show love to those around you?

I recommend that you get hold of a copy of "the 5 Love Languages", by Gary Chapman. Essentially, Gary Chapman suggests people have a preferred way of loving and being loved – we all have our primary "love languages". The book also suggests that we all have a love tank, which can be topped up or depleted. In simple terms, when you speak your partner's love language, you top up their love tank. When you neglect speaking their language, their tank is depleted.

The five languages that Chapman identifies are:

Quality time

If your primary love language is quality time you will appreciate it when loved ones spend time with you, giving you their full attention. Quality time might mean doing a joint hobby, or perhaps putting aside time each day to connect in conversation (and listening) or by doing something together.

If your primary language is quality time, then you may find it frustrating to be told, "you go ahead and do that by yourself", or you feel you are being ignored and not listened to. If your partner is always too busy to find time to spend connecting with you, your love tank will be depleted.

Acts of service

If your primary love language is acts of service, you will feel loved when your partner does things for you. Perhaps he/she makes you a cup of tea every morning or empties the dishwasher when you feel tired after a challenging day at work. Or maybe they rub your shoulders when they ache or have dinner ready when you've been at work since 6am.

If your primary language is acts of service you may find your love tank is depleted when you feel that everything is falling to you to do, when your partner is not pulling their weight, or doesn't see when you feel tired and could do with a break.

Words of affirmation

If words of affirmation are your thing, then you will feel loved when your partner tells you how much they love and value you, writes you a card telling you how they feel, or gives you positive and encouraging feedback. You will probably feel loved when you feel appreciated and thanked for the things you do.

On the other hand, if your partner doesn't often say they love you or tell you that they care and appreciate you, that will hurt and your love tank will fall.

Gifts

Some of you will probably feel loved when your partner buys you things, and thinks of you when they see something they know you would like. The gifts don't always have to be big or expensive, but they show thoughtfulness and that you are cared for.

If your primary love language is gifts, then it will really hurt if your partner forgets your birthday or neglects to get you a Valentines' gift.

Physical touch

If your primary love language is physical touch, then you will love it when your partner touches you lightly as they pass, or gives you a cuddle, or holds your hand while you walk side by side. Physical touch isn't all about sex – it's about connecting through touch.

You won't like it when they forget to kiss you goodbye or withdraw that affection after an argument.

Which love languages do you speak most fluently?

Which love languages?

Spend some time considering which of these languages means the most to you.

Some editions of Gary Chapman's book include a quiz at the back to help you identify which language matters most to you, or you could search online to find the quiz to answer.

You will probably find that two or three of them stand out as most important. Mine, for example are acts of service, physical touch and words of affirmation. If I receive all of those in my relationship, I feel loved, valued and appreciated. My love tank is full.

Most of us will automatically express love to our partner in the way we like to be shown it – in the love languages we are most comfortable with. If you want to really understand how to best show love to your partner, start to look for clues as to your partner's love language, and use their language to show them your love. This is easy if it is a language that comes naturally to you and may take some effort if it isn't.

Whenever you enter a new relationship, why not set an intention to be open to noticing clues as to your partner's preferred love languages? Have a discussion with your new partner about your preferred language. As the relationship develops, notice whether your needs are being met. Perhaps keep a metaphorical love tank in your mind and check in every so often how 'topped up' it feels.

Know what you want!

After my divorce, the first person I became romantically involved with was the exact opposite of my ex-husband in almost all ways. Where my ex liked a drink, he drank very little. While my ex-husband was very sociable and always the last person standing at the bar at a party, he preferred an early night and could take or leave social occasions. Even physically there were opposites - my ex is tall, and he was not. I naively thought that by going for someone who was the opposite of my ex, I would get exactly what I wanted. How wrong was I?! That relationship eventually ended in tears, and I realised that there were some aspects of my ex-husband that were valuable to me.

It is tempting to do what I did and assume that the opposite of your ex is exactly what you need. However, the fact that your relationship with your ex is now over doesn't mean that everything about him or her was wrong for you. Even though you are no longer together, and they may have hurt you along the way, you are now in a place to evaluate the relationship and learn from it.

- Were there any aspects of your ex that you really appreciated?
- Were there others that you would avoid in future?

I often help clients to describe their ideal future partner. This exercise is similar to one that Sara Davison shared with me during our training. When we went through it on the course, I realised that this was almost exactly the process I had used to describe and identify my now-husband, 4 years earlier!

I believe that once you know what you are looking for, you will be more likely to see it when it is in front of you. When you know what you are focusing on, often it presents itself.

My future partner

Take a large piece of paper, and on it brainstorm all the qualities, attributes and characteristics that you would look for in any future partner. Take your time and forget about what you think might be "realistic".

Write down anything that is important to you, for example:

- What do they look like?
- How tall are they?
- Do they have children? How old are they?
- What interests do they have?
- What do they like doing in their spare time?
- What qualities MUST they have?
- What values do you want them to hold?
- What sort of job do they do?

Make sure that you phrase these attributes in positive language, so that they aren't a list of things you don't want. Rather than "isn't interested in cars", or "doesn't love shopping", write down what you DO want, so that might be "interested in learning to dance" or "loves walking in the woods". Make your list positive, specific and clear.

Once you have a clear picture of what you do want, consider whether there are any "absolute no's". These are the non-negotiable things that mean that this person is absolutely not right for you. What will you not accept? Narrow these down to a maximum of 3-5. I say this because although these "absolute no's" are non-negotiable, the main point of this exercise is to focus on what you DO want, and what is truly important to you in a partner.

When I was dating again after that first disastrous relationship, I decided that any future partner I had must be kind, funny and gentle. He had to be single and available, willing to accept my children, and he had to enjoy dancing, or be willing to learn. He also had to be healthy and fit and keen to try new things, travel and explore with me. I wanted him to have grown up children, rather than young ones. There was a lot more on my list, and when I showed it to one of my friends, she laughed and said I'd never be able to find anyone like that. She was wrong!

Once you have your list, you can keep going back to it, refining it, and using it as a benchmark to check in with whenever you meet anyone. You could also create a vision board with pictures and images that reflect the qualities and attributes you are looking for.

When you know what it is you are looking for, you are more likely to recognise it when it presents itself. Having a compelling vision of what you want will mean that you can quickly assess whether someone is right for you or not.

Stepping out into the world of creating new relationships can feel daunting at first. However,

when you know who you are, what you want, and
what you will and won't accept, you are well equipped
to make the most of the opportunities that will come
your way.

CHAPTER 21

Moving Forward
with Confidence
and Choice

Right at the start of this book, I offered you hope, and a promise that you will feel better, that there is light at the end of the tunnel. I promised to hold the belief for you that that you can feel happy again, the knowledge that you can get over your heartbreak, and feel back in control of your life and future until you are ready to step into it yourself. I hope that you have found tools in this book to help you do just that.

When I look back, my recovery from my sudden break-up and subsequent divorce is one of my proudest achievements. I look back and know that I did my very best, and that I couldn't have handled it any better. There were of course days when I felt truly bereft and distressed, but over time, and by using the techniques I've shared with you in this book, those days became fewer and fewer, and more infrequent. This is what I want for you, too.

Clients often ask me if what they are feeling is "normal", and many don't believe when we first meet that they will ever feel better. I hope that by using the strategies in this book, you have seen that you can feel better, and you can put yourself back in the driving seat of your life by making conscious decisions to do things differently, look for choices, and keep your focus firmly on you. The book is designed for you to dip in and out of the chapters that are relevant to you at any particular time, and quickly find the exercises and techniques I share.

I know that going through a sudden break-up can feel very lonely, so I hope that I have been able to show you that you are not alone, and that there are many things you can do to see things from a different perspective, or in a different light, so that you can find the upside. I often compare the dark times of a break-up to feeling as though you have fallen into a dark, cold, damp well. What you need in those times is someone with a ladder to help you climb back out. You don't need someone to climb in with you and join you sitting in the pool of water at the bottom. This book, along with the support of all those people in your support team, is intended to be a ladder to give you the tools to climb back out. Sometimes you may take a step or two back down, but the ladder is always there for you.

I can't promise you that you will never again have a low day or feel challenged by the road ahead. I can't promise you that life won't throw you another curve ball. What I can promise you is that you now have access to a toolkit of strategies and ways of shifting your perception that can help you to turn things around, and handle anything that may happen to you in the future!

I know how deeply a sudden break-up can affect you – mine rocked me to my core, and made me question everything I had believed in, including myself and my own worth. Now, though, I have a deep belief in my ability to handle whatever life may throw at me. That belief gives me a real sense of calm and confidence, and I can feel it like a light inside. Whatever happens, I know I have strategies to handle it and to find a way through. Sometimes, it is the worst times of our lives that challenge us to step up and handle things we never even believed possible. And when you notice how you overcome each challenge, big or small, you build up your belief in your own ability to handle anything.

When you feel yourself sliding back into those darker moments or days, come back to this book and go back through your favourite techniques. They are designed to be used again and again. Re-read all your post-it notes and affirmations and remind yourself that you can do it. Refocus, regroup, and remember to notice when you do something that works. Choose a technique that works for you and use it. Every time you practice any of the techniques, they become more natural and you'll be taking small steps in a positive way towards the future that you deserve.

Finally, there are three things I want you to really take to heart:

Remember that it is not what happens to you that makes the difference, it is what you do with what happens to you.

You always have choices about how you react, how you feel and what you do, and those choices are what will define your life.

**And, dear reader, remember you deserve to be happy. You are good enough.
You can do this.**

Thank you for buying my book – it has been written with the intention of helping as many people as possible to recover from a sudden break-up and find their own strength and power to create a new and vibrant life. I hope that you have found it useful and easy to navigate, and that it has given you comfort, hope and a knowledge that you can do it.

Whatever you choose to do, wherever you choose to go, whoever you choose to become, I wish you all the happiness you deserve.

CHAPTER 22

Client Stories

Caroline's story

Caroline got in touch with me after her husband of over 30 years left her very suddenly for someone else, who was a lot younger than either Caroline or her husband. Caroline told me she felt heartbroken, betrayed and very angry. She was struggling to hold it together at work and felt that her house was no longer her home. She described herself as rudderless and lost, and she was scared of being alone.

During our time together, Caroline learnt that she could take back control over her feelings and find a way forward that meant she could rebuild her confidence and start to plan for her future. I showed her ways in which she could dial down her fears and worries, and channel her anger into focusing on herself and her recovery. Although she couldn't always control the situation, and she certainly couldn't control what her ex-husband did or said, she was able to start to take back her power over her own emotions, her home and work environments, and her future. Through taking small steps over every day during the next weeks and months, Caroline was able to transform how she saw and experienced her separation.

Since I first spoke to her, when she was nervous about driving to meet me in my coaching room, Caroline has travelled by herself to the Far East and the US, handled the curveballs that her separation has thrown her with dignity and a quiet strength, and she has been promoted at work – a promotion that she had been offered before her separation, but turned down as she didn't feel confident enough to take it.

She has a long list of 'firsts' that she has achieved over the last year, and I will never forget the Friday night I received a message from her saying that she was smiling to herself as she checked into her flight online, as this was another 'first' for her, and she felt proud and pleased at how much she had grown.

Caroline has changed completely over the time we have worked together. Her family and friends have commented on all the differences they have noticed in her. Although at the time I write, Caroline's divorce is still in progress, she knows now that she has the resilience and strength to deal with it, and to plan a new future for herself.

I am so proud of Caroline and how much she achieved over the months we worked together. It is a wonderful feeling to see a client move from feeling devastated by a loss that came out of the blue, to taking charge of her everyday life bit by bit, and rediscover what Caroline herself calls "being truly me".

Emily's story

"I don't think I could have attended mediation with my ex-husband without Claire's help to battle my anxiety. Claire gave me confidence and helped me find strength to deal with an extremely upsetting situation, when I was feeling helpless, broken and unable to go on."

Emily first came to see me after her solicitor recommended me to her. Emily had been married for 10 years, and with her husband for 20. They had one daughter together, who was 8. Like Caroline, Emily's husband had left for another woman a few months earlier, leaving Emily and their daughter very upset, confused, in debt and with a half-completed house project underway. Emily's husband had admitted previously to having several affairs during their marriage, and Emily was full of anger and resentment at the time she saw as having been wasted. She was also angry for their daughter, and reluctant to allow any contact between their daughter and her ex-husband's new girlfriend.

Emily also felt that her husband was behaving in an aggressive and controlling way towards her. She felt that he directed a lot of blame and hostility towards her. He was withholding information from her solicitor and at the same time insisting that they attend mediation, which made Emily feel highly anxious, confused and fearful. Emily was struggling to sleep and eat, and her emotional strength was drained. Although she had friends and family around, she felt that she was dealing with the situation very much on her own, and she felt that the divorce was happening to her. She knew that she needed some help in order to protect herself and her daughter emotionally. She wanted to get some clarity on the way forward and feel able to resolve the situation and finalise the divorce.

Emily is an amazing woman, with huge reserves of strength and resilience that she could draw on, and together we worked to remind her of her inner strength, so that she could draw on it when she needed to. We worked on a series of steps that Emily could take to prepare mentally for mediation, which she was able to attend successfully, and eventually even to meet her ex-husband's girlfriend. She found that, during those meetings, she was able to identify when her anxiety levels were rising and use techniques we developed together to stay calm. She was able to articulate her views and boundaries without her emotions taking over.

Emily now describes herself as feeling confident that she can deal with anything being thrown at her, and she is stronger, happier and more hopeful for the future. She is able to react calmly to emails and correspondence from her ex-husband and his solicitor.

Emily has also found that the strategies we developed together have helped her to support her daughter with her feelings too. She listens to her emotions, worries and concerns, and is able to support her effectively.

"I am rediscovering the person I was before my marriage: a fierce, strong & independent woman, who doesn't take cr*p from anyone. I feel like myself again. I am stronger, more confident and reassured that I can deal with anything now."

Jodie's story

Jodie first got in touch a couple of months after her husband had left out of the blue. She was facing a lot of decisions about her future and was unsure which way to turn. She felt overwhelmed by the process in front of her and she was worried about the potential impact of the separation on their children. She was confused and heartbroken but putting on a brave face and trying to muddle through. She also felt angry and betrayed, and she knew that she wanted to feel differently.

I showed Jodie how to turn down the temperature on her emotions and start to see her interactions with her ex-husband differently, including accepting that she couldn't control his responses and actions; only her own. Her anger softened and she was able to see the upsides in her situation.

Jodie found that when she looked for different choices in any situation, she could find clarity and confidence. Initially, the choices she made were around issues like what to do with some of her ex-husband's possessions which remained in the house, and how to handle parents' evening appointments at school. As time went on, Jodie found that she could make more and more decisions with confidence and clarity, taking charge of her busy mind, and stopping her imagination running away with her.

Jodie was worried about what to tell people who asked her how she was, or who made comments about her divorce, which had been a surprise for many of her friends. We worked out a handful of great responses that Jodie could practice and start to use. She felt her confidence and strength growing and pulling her forward.

Jodie is a wonderfully creative woman, with a talent for visualising her dreams. Together we created a vision for her new home and life, which gave her focus and meant that she could believe that her most heartfelt hopes could become her new reality. She created action plans full of small steps that would take her closer to her dreams and committed to taking those steps. She now knows that she is braver than she thought, and she can accomplish anything she chooses.

Luke's story

When Luke first came to see me, he had already been divorced for several years, but was struggling to move forward. He felt that he was stuck in the past, constantly thinking about what he had lost in terms of his marriage, family and finances. He felt he had very little hope for a positive future and described himself as stuck in a spiral of negativity. He felt that he was not good enough, and his relationship with his children was suffering. He felt strongly that he had been a victim of his divorce, and found his thoughts going in circles of "why did it happen to me?" and "what did I do wrong?".

Over our time together, Luke began to believe that there were other options available to him. He saw himself from the perspective of his children, and he understood how his negativity was impacting on them. He remembered the good fun dad he had been previously and started to organise activities to bring that side of himself back out. When his son commented on the difference, Luke felt proud and invigorated.

Luke often felt anxious and judged, and he didn't believe he was good enough. We explored what he really loved to do and was good at, and he began to see himself through a different lens. He started to look for and notice the good things in his life. He saw that he had determination and tenacity, and that he had the ability to make other people laugh. He found that by getting out, following his passion for outdoor sports and engaging with people and activities that made him happy, his perception of himself shifted, and he could see the talents he had to offer. Now, he volunteers for a charity supporting children to get more involved in sport.

As Luke grew in confidence and self-belief, he found that his pattern of negative thinking no longer served him. He made a conscious effort to interrupt any spiralling thought patterns and replace them with better questions and positivity. His energy levels rose, and he began to focus his efforts towards pursuing the paths and options he wanted to follow in the future, rather than dwelling on the past.

Previously, he had always believed that he could only have one thing or the other – now he looks for ways to achieve both and believes that he can. His confidence has increased, and he is proud of who he is, and what he has to offer. His mindset when faced with a challenge has shifted totally and he knows that he is as deserving of success and happiness as everyone else.

Acknowledgements

I have so many people to thank, without whom this book would not have been possible, and who were integral to my support team while I was going through my divorce.

Firstly, my family who rushed down from Surrey to Bristol in the middle of the night – Mum, Dad and my brother Richard. For many months, Mum phoned me every day to check in, until eventually I said I really was OK and no longer needed her to!

To all my wonderful friends who saw me through many a dark hour, both in person and in long telephone calls. Keeley, who opened up her home for many weekends in the early days and was always ready to listen. Sam, who provided more breakfasts than I could count when I wasn't really eating. Cathy, who sent supportive messages all the way from New Zealand. Jelly, my oldest school friend, whose Reiki treatment gave me my first full night's sleep and Bev, who I 'met' on Mumsnet and who became a pivotal part of my recovery through our email correspondence. And my neighbours, Janet and Nigel, who provided many a cup of tea, and who helped me formulate an action plan when I needed things to look forward to.

My work colleagues at Berwin Leighton Paisner LLP, as it was then, were endlessly patient and kind with me, especially David, Kirsty and Sophie. I will never forget the support I received from all of you.

I have been lucky enough to train with fabulous teachers and mentors, including Neil Almond and Andy Cartmell of 91 Untold in Bristol, and Sara Davison, the Divorce Coach. You have all taught me so much. Jools Parsons was my life-coach after I decided to leave the legal world, and she helped me to plan, set up and start my business. She held the belief and knowledge that I could do it before I did! Also Rob Carter, the business coach who keeps me on the straight and narrow, and always asks incisive questions to challenge my thinking. I have been surrounded by fantastic NLP colleagues at every stage of my journey, notably Michelle Eichenberger, Jolanta Valeniece and Jed Lazar – who first challenged me to write a book.

Thank you also to Ann Hobbs of Forward Thinking Publishing, who has done a wonderful job of editing and publishing, to enable me to bring my vision for this book to life. And to Lisa Ravenscroft at Longmoose Graphics for the brilliant cover design, which truly reflects the positive feeling of forward motion that I described to her, all whilst using my favourite dragonflies.

And of course, thank you to all the clients I have worked with since Claire Black Coaching was born. It has been a pleasure and a privilege to work with all of you.

My love and thanks go to my wonderful children, Laurie and Fraser, without whom I might not have got out of bed in the early days, and who are growing into fine young men of whom I am immensely proud. And Paul, my lovely husband, who has supported me throughout, who has always believed I could do it, and who encouraged me to take the first steps towards creating my dream. I love you!

About the Author

Claire Black's marriage broke down very suddenly in 2008 when her husband told her he was having an affair and left their marriage. Her experience of overcoming the heartache and challenges that this threw up ultimately led her to a change of career, from City Lawyer to Break-up and Divorce Coach.

Early on in her own break-up, Claire decided that she was not going to allow her divorce to define her negatively. Instead, she came to see it as an opportunity to get to know herself again and create a new future for herself and her children. Her divorce now defines her in a different way – as one of the UK's leading Break-up and Divorce Coaches.

When her marriage ended, Break-up and Divorce coaching did not exist in the UK, and Claire found it challenging to find non-judgmental, impartial guidance that focused on moving forward rather than looking back at what went wrong. Claire found her own way through, fuelled by a strong determination to be "dignified at all times", and an overriding desire to do the very best she could for her children. She created her coaching business so that she could support others to access their own strength and resilience, so that they too can feel proud when they look back.

Claire is a Master NLP Practitioner, having trained for 18 months with 91 Untold in Bristol. She also completed specialist training with Sara Davison, the Divorce Coach. She is also a qualified solicitor, although she no longer practises. Claire brings all her personal and professional expertise to every coaching session, so that she can be the best coach she can be for each and every client.

Above all, Claire wants anyone going through a sudden break-up to know that they are not alone, and that there is hope.

If you would like to work more closely with Claire, you can do that in a number of ways, through individual coaching or by attending one of her workshops. If you would like more information, please visit Claire's website at www.claireblackcoaching.com, where you can also download copies of many of the techniques in this book.

You can also find Claire on Facebook, Linkedin and Twitter, links below, where she posts regularly with tips and hints to help you keep your focus positive and on you.

www.claireblackcoaching.com

https://www.facebook.com/ClaireBlackDivorceCoaching/

https://www.linkedin.com/in/claire-black-divorce-coach/

https://twitter.com/CBDivorceCoach

Further Reading

Misfit to Maven – Ebonie Allard

The Five Love Languages – Gary Chapman

When Things Fall Apart – Pema Chodron

Uncoupled – Sara Davison

Man's Search for Meaning – Viktor Frankl

Feel the Fear and do it anyway – Susan Jeffers

The Divorce Doctor – Francine Kaye

I can mend your broken heart - Paul McKenna and Hugh Willbourn